Reflections With God While Waiting To Be Healed

Linda Seger, Th.D.

Clovercroft Publishing

Reflections With God While Waiting to be Healed

Published by Clovercroft Publishing, Franklin, Tennessee

Published in association with Larry Carpenter of Christian Book Services, LLC.
www.christianbookservices.com

Cover Design by Nick Zelinger

Interior Design by Suzanne Lawing

Edited by Lapiz Digital Services

Printed in the United States of America

978-1-942557-70-8

Endorsements For
Reflections With God While Waiting To Be Healed

Perhaps one of the hardest things to endure when one is battling a chronic illness is coming to terms with how intensely personal, lonely and unique one's suffering is. Most people untested by this kind of trouble cannot relate well. In fact, most are frightened or repelled by such pain as though it might be catching to stand too close. In "Reflections with God", readers who are battling illness will find a kindred spirit in Linda, a soul so tested in the crucible of affliction she is qualified to voice the haunting questions, doubts, agonies, and fears about life, loss, the unknown, and the very character and motives of God. Not only will readers be comforted by her profound compassion and empathy, but also be rewarded—perhaps even transformed—by this intensely personal journey towards light and healing, and the gradual discovery of a new order of profound and satisfying depths.

—**MARION MACKENZIE PYLE**
   Author, *Healed, Healthy and Whole, How We Beat Cancer with Integrative Therapies and Essential Healing Strategies*

"While "waiting to be healed," in her Reflections With God, Linda Seger offers to others walking a similarly arduous path of prolonged chronic illness, the hope and comfort of a highly evolved, intentional spirituality. This is not the route of superficial theology, of pat answers to demanding challenges. Rather, it is the Way of the Cross, the way that acknowledges the reality of the human condition of pain and suffering, doubt and despair, while holding fast to, "clinging to," the ultimate promise that God's will for us is wholeness and health. In the strong embrace of that promise Dr. Seger's reflections encourage others to find serenity within the wait, as she has."

—THE REV. CN. JEAN PARKER VAIL, D.MIN.
    Author, *In the Name of God: Exploring God's Love in Prayer and Pulpit*

"As a fellow sufferer of Dystonia, Linda Seger has given a unique perspective on God's role in life when a chronic illness interrupts a life that seems to be on such a promising path. Suddenly and without warning illness can strike and we ask God for his intervention. Are his plans for our future the same as our own? 'I find this book refreshing and adding another angle to my outlook on God and his role in my life!"

—BRENDA CURREY LEWIS
    Author, *A Twisted Fate: My Life with Dystonia*

"This book is a very personal sorting out of theology, self-awareness, and one's body. Does illness have meaning and how is that understanding to be used in getting well? What new and old ideas will help one cope with the changes/challenges that we fear? What manner of faith helps or hinders as we try to live lives in new directions? Can old assumptions be scrubbed up to help us into new patterns? Personal theology under threat of illness is a good place of much homework and this book is a fine example of that particular seeking."

—JOHN CALVI
Author, *The Dance Between Hope and Fear*

"Waiting. Watching. Wounded. Wondering. Sick of being sick of being sick. "Reflections with God While Waiting to Be Healed" is a treasure of insights on pain, fear and hope for anyone on a journey through the uncertainty of illness and all who love them but don't know what to say or do."

—REV. DR. RICH MELHEIM
Founder, www.faithink.com

"What a book! What wisdom, what insights! Linda's story is so moving; she embraces her illnesses in ways that are unique and healthy, hopeful and positive, brutally honest and without "answers". She explores life in 360 degrees: physically, emotionally, spiritually, morally, intellectually, and creatively.

Illness can clarify one's life. It has for Linda. She lays out the human condition in simple terms that will take the reader to new ways of understanding and will lead to becoming whole in ways one might not anticipate. Even for those who don't suffer, these thoughts and struggles will enrich them.

Linda's journey has not been easy. As others also dream, she wishes for a miracle but doesn't waste time simply hoping for that without taking steps for her healing.

Her background and education and creativity combine to create a book that will stand the test of time; it challenges the reader to live a fuller life. "Reflections" is a tool to deal with stress and to move to a more peaceful, spiritual, and calm place. This book is good for the soul."

—RON RUBIN
Manager, Colorado Springs Memorial Hospital Foundation

Dedicated to Dr. Gail Henry,
who gave me hope and a future.

Acknowledgments

Thank you:

To Dr. Gail Henry, my chiropractic neurologist from Houston, Texas, for her brilliance, her constant care, and commitment to my healing.

To Dr. Michaele Sparaco-Posey, my chiropractic neurologist in Colorado Springs, Colorado, for encouraging me, maintaining me, and her constant support and desire for me to be healed.

To Dr. Sunumu Ikeda, associate doctor in Houston, Texas, for his technical proficiency at ordering my neurons to behave well, and for all his kindness and care.

To Dr. Matthew Antonucci, Dr. Kelsey Brenner, and Jamie Norman at The Brain Plasticity Center in Orlando, Florida.

To my readers: Wendy Barzelay, Devorah Cutler-Rubenstein, Diane Kalmajian, Peter Le Var, Brenda Currey Lewis, Cathleen Loeser, Nancy Perala, Pauline Sateran, Pamela Jaye Smith, Brenda Winn, and my Bible consultant and prayer partner, Linda Crawford, for their feedback and help.

To the many friends, neighbors, and relatives who have been so supportive of me through both dystonia and cancer.

To my therapists, and various assistants, in Houston: Enrique, Tomas, Jessica, Mandy, Greg, Sonia, Yaily, Pui, and Chloe.

Thank you to my oncology doctors, Dr. Laura Pomeranke, Dr. Jane Ridings, Doctor Uchenna Njiaju, and Dr. Britta Mutti.

And thank you to my radiation therapists: Michael, Kathy, Kim, Kevin, Rebecca, and Ramona. To my physical therapists in Colorado Springs: Andrea, Kristin, and Janelle. They not only have done good work, but have understood all the psychological nuances of illness. They have cheered me on.

To Sister Therese of Benet Hill Monastery, my spiritual director.

To my assistant, Katie Gardner, for her reliability and good work, kindness, and feedback on the book.

To my dear husband, Peter Le Var, for his notes, his constant care and support in sickness and in health, and his devotion to me and my work.

Foreword

Dr. Michaele M. Sparaco-Posey

I remember the first time I saw Linda. She was not yet my patient, but it was very apparent that she needed help. It was in 2008 that I had my first interactions with her and it would be several years before we would cross paths again. I was sitting in my office one day when the phone rang. The voice I heard on the other end was one of excitement, apprehension and nervousness when she asked me if I was the Dr. Sparaco she had met several years ago. When I replied yes, the emotion in her voice was palpable and she asked me for my first available appointment. To my surprise, Linda came to her appointment vastly improved from the last time I had seen her. She let me know that she had found Dr. Gail Henry in Houston and had been working with her for the past few years.

And so our journey began. I have been witness to many beautiful moments during Linda's journey, but what has always been steadfast throughout her experiences was her faith and commitment to allow God to lead her towards healing. There is simply no other reason for her to have found me again after so many years had passed since our initial interactions.

Dystonia is not an easy disorder in which to live. The physical, emotional and mental toll it takes is not describable. Linda writes herein that she finds courage in my office. Often times that is the hardest part of the journey. The first time Linda told me that she feels courage after she leaves my office I thought my heart would explode, because at that very moment I knew that I was taking care of a fighter. I firmly believe that true courage comes from within. It comes from the deep seeded ability to face life's challenges with grace and dignity while facing fear without reservation.

One of my favorite authors writes:

> **"I shall be telling this with a sigh**
> **Somewhere ages and ages hence:**
> **Two roads diverged in a wood, and I-**
> **I took the one less traveled by,**
> **And that has made all the difference"**
> -*The Road Less Traveled* by Robert Frost

Linda's story has been defined by taking the road less traveled. She has sought out some of the world's best doctors and foremost experts on dystonia. Functional Neurologists are premier, elite doctors specializing in treating some of the most complex of conditions. We have the pleasure of offering unique and individualized treatment protocols for conditions that may otherwise have a questionable outcome. We're out there, eager to help with every aspect of healing. Linda, thankfully found us and is completely committed to regaining her health and well being. The brain and body connection is undeniable, and those that acknowledge that there is something more than meets the eye concerning the brain have a unique advantage on the road to health.

Linda has set forth a prime example of courage, strength and conviction for us all to follow in any of life's struggles. Use her story and example to find comfort in any struggle you may encounter. It has been an honor to be a part of this team; to know Linda personally and walk this path to health with her. I will never doubt that God led her to my steps and gifted me with the talents to be a part of her journey.

And so the journey continues...

Contents

Introduction

It was a happy life! I had a successful international business as a script consultant in the film industry, gave seminars on screenwriting around the world, and was the author of almost a dozen books. My husband and I had moved to my dream house in my dream state of Colorado in 2002. And I had finally bought a horse, after wanting one since I was 13 years old.

Then in 2008, something changed my course of happiness. My head began to turn to the left, involuntarily. At first, I simply observed it. It would turn all the way to the left and I would turn it back. Three seconds later, it would turn again. I asked my husband, who is a massage therapist and acupuncturist, "What is this?" He didn't know what it was and suggested that I go to a massage therapist who specialized in medical conditions. While I lay on Bonnie's massage table, she said to me, "This isn't muscular. This is neurological." She sent me to a chiropractic neurologist. Within two months, I had a diagnosis: it's called *cervical dystonia*, or *spasmodic torticolis,* a movement disorder where the brain sends the wrong message to the muscle. The brain doesn't seem to understand where center is, and it thinks that it has to rebalance itself in one direction. In my case, the movement was to the left, but with this condition, it can be up and down or it can be to the right as well. I went to a neurologist, had an MRI, but everything within the brain was normal except for this message that somehow was not getting through correctly to my neck muscle. Why did this suddenly happen? The doctor said it's usually the result of a physical trauma that happens three to five months before the onset of symptoms. I couldn't think of any trauma that I had, until I remembered I had been a passenger in a small car accident a few months before. 'Was that enough?" He said, "Yes."

"So, what are my choices and how do I get better?" The neurologist suggested the usual protocol that is done in a case like this—a Botox shot. The Botox shot doesn't cure it, and within a few months the Botox wears off and the ritual starts all over again. I said to the doctor, "So you want me to have a shot of Botox in my neck every three months for the rest of my life?" He replied, "Yes." I thought about it for a moment and then said, "This doesn't seem like a good idea." I didn't just want relief; I wanted to be healed. After further research, I realized once I started down that route I wouldn't be able to reverse course because the toxins from Botox would cause other problems.

I wondered, "Was there another alternative?" I tried a number of things: physical therapy, upper cervical spine manipulation by a chiropractor, Reiki massage therapy, acupuncture, visualizations, and biofeedback. Clearly, nothing was working. After almost nine months of trying to figure out what to do, my friend Pamela Jaye Smith said to me, "Somewhere in the world there's an expert on this condition. Go find that person!" My friend, Lynn Rosenberg, researched the world for me to find someone who could help me and discovered a chiropractic neurologist in Houston, Texas who had some success with patients who have this condition.

Not only is this condition aggravating and frustrating and uncomfortable, but it interferes with so many good aspects of life. When trying to sleep, my head begins turning. Upon awakening, I can't doze or think good thoughts about the day, or lie in bed with my husband and talk or listen—because my head is turning almost immediately upon waking. When sitting down closing my eyes to pray or meditate, my head starts turning and I have to focus on turning my head back to center. This was one of the worst results because praying to ask for help is almost impossible due to the constant distraction. I finally simply talked my prayer with my eyes open, although this didn't give me the peace I usually had.

When watching a movie I have to sit to the left of the screen so I'm facing right, because otherwise the neck strains. When I go out to dinner to eat with friends they need to be on my right side, which has occasionally caused problems when the friend is deaf in the left ear and needs me to be on the right side!

Most people who see me don't realize I have this condition. The head turns at rest, and when I'm turning it during the day, it looks quite natural.

It is now almost seven years later. There is improvement. I've been doing two to four hours of therapy a day all these years. At this point, instead of my head turning to the left 70 degrees, it sometimes only turns 1 to 5 degrees. Sometimes it takes a position of slightly off-center.

Sometimes it's calm and stays neutral. The doctors believe full recovery will come, but like many neurological problems, nothing happens quickly.

Then, in 2015, as I felt I had made real progress with dystonia, I was diagnosed with early stage breast cancer. I didn't need chemotherapy, but had twenty sessions of radiation, and then started taking the cancer pill—but had so many drastic side effects I couldn't continue. Now I'm working with supplements and diet to reduce my chances of a recurrence.

The journey toward healing raises many spiritual questions. They're not just questions of faith or just questions of theology or just questions of our relationship with God. They're questions about where the Spirit is leading us and why we have to go there.

This book is written from the viewpoint of a person who is a Christian and a Quaker and who has studied theology. I believe these ideas and issues are universal, and many people from other spiritual disciplines may resonate with these ideas. In the 1970s, after receiving an M.A. in Drama, I went to seminary and received a master's degree in Religion and the Arts and then a Th.D. in Drama and Theology. Later I received an M.A. in Feminist Theology. I've spent my adult career as a script consultant, speaker, and author in the area of screenwriting, focusing on my drama background while integrating spiritual perspectives into my work. I also write books on spirituality and have worked on developing my spiritual life.

In this journey, I've been blessed to have a spiritual director who is a Catholic nun, Sister Therese, my doctors Dr. Henry and Dr. Sparaco-Posey, who are spiritual, and many, many friends who have given me wisdom and perspective and insight and support and great encouragement. I also have a very loving, caring, and compassionate spouse (my dear Peter) who has been willing to do anything needed to help me.

So many of us go through physical and mental problems. Few people are without some area in their life that needs healing. Many of these problems are hidden from our view, yet they're a daily edge in the person's life. At times on this journey, I have looked at various people and said to myself, "That's one person that doesn't have a problem. Their life looks great and they look physically and mentally happy." Oh, I have been very wrong in most cases! Almost everyone's life takes a tumble.

I hope this book speaks to the many people who are dealing with illnesses that might be cured or illnesses that may never be cured. I believe these issues are relevant to anybody who has a spiritual slant on life. May this book give you insights, encouragement, wisdom, new perceptions, new reflections and may it serve your healing journey.

PART ONE:

Questions, Concerns, and Struggles

CHAPTER 1:

Wanting To Be Healed

The wish for healing has always been half of health
—Lucius Annaeus Seneca

Everybody wants us to be healed. Doctors work feverishly to make their cure work. Friends search for something that will help, "Have you tried this? Have you tried that? If you tried this heat pillow, would that help? What about that faith healer or this doctor or that form of therapy?" They believe that there is an answer to whatever it is that's wrong with us. Relatives wish us well and are concerned that this might happen to them and wonder if it's genetic or contagious.

But beneath all the desires for wellness, there is an underlying understanding from our loved ones and our medical team that our illness is not how things are supposed to be. They want us to be happy, to be whole, and to be healed.

We might experience all their goodwill as a burden because their advice is asking us to do more than what we're already doing. They suggest another phone call to make, another therapy to research. Yet, we're already exhausted and just barely hanging on. Their concern is meant as encouragement, but we wonder if we can live up to the hope that they're trying to give us. We might feel their desire for healing is forcing us to reach for something that just doesn't seem possible.

In the midst of a sense of being overwhelmed, we might stop believing in our purpose for living. Some might wonder where God is in this chaotic world. Often we're told that life is supposed to be abundant, to be perfect and in harmony. We're told God is supportive of who we are and what we dream of and wants to help us achieve our full potential. But it's not working out as we hoped, and as we thought God wanted.

From a spiritual perspective, the underlying question is often: "What does God want from us? What is the possibility for our future? And, do we have a future? Is it possible that our illness is God's will? Where is the Holy Spirit in all this?"

We might ask, "Why? Why is this happening to me since I have the faith to believe that I'm a beloved child of God? Is there a reason I don't yet understand?"

But we might also ask, "Why not?" Why should we escape the flaws and difficulties and struggles when so many others are ailing? Why should we be untouched by the vulnerability at the heart of all human life? Are we victims of the flawed human condition even though we've escaped these problems until now? Is this supposed to have meaning, and am I capable of finding it?

CHAPTER 2:

Changing Our Theology

Faith is a knowledge of the heart
beyond the reach of proof
—Khalil Gibran

Occasionally someone who is ill may be blessed with a philosophy of life which already leaves room for its trials and tribulations. In one way or another, they have at least some of the patterns of life figured out and have formed a spiritual approach to life (a theology) about who God is, who we are, and what the meaning of it all is.

I know people of great faith who see themselves so clearly as a child of God that they have a beautiful trust that all is in the hands of God and that, underneath all their struggles, that Presence upholds them. Some believe illness is an opportunity to bring us closer to God and reflect on our lives in new ways. Some simply surrender.

Some people accept their illness as God's will—or at least all is in God's hands. My sister Holly was like this when she was diagnosed with ALS (Lou Gehrig's Disease.) She lived and died with acceptance and grace and courage, believing in God's love and timing. I often wish I could be like her.

One of my doctors, Dr. Sparaco-Posey, told me she has patients like this although she smiled and admitted that didn't define her—or me.

Many of us struggle with issues and argue and discuss with God. Unexpected problems can upset our theology and nothing seems to fit. We have questions that are not easily answered because the situation has forced us to change the way we look at things.

Sometimes an illness can undermine our belief systems and throw into doubt a faith we have spent years building up and believing in. It compromises our ability to trust. Suddenly, we wonder if God is anywhere near or in any way cares.

We struggle to affirm our theology or to expand our ideas about God. We might grapple with the meaning of what has sustained us in the past but now comes into question. And sometimes in that struggle, something shifts and expands.

Many of us might have a spiritual belief system that includes the problem of evil and the problem of our human flaws. But we may not have had it tested to the extent that our injuries are testing us. When we become ill, our illness may not seem to fit into the scheme of things. Our theology sees a healing God, one who wishes the best for us and loves us and cares for us. Our theology might have a belief that when we pray, we're connecting with this Almighty

God and Most Holy Spirit. We presume a miracle will happen if we pray and hold steady and perhaps go to church more and do good things.

There are many, many verses in Scripture and also in other spiritual writings about healing and there are many promises and presumptions that, if we pray, God will come to our aid. Yet here we are, suffering with an illness, having to deal with physical and mental wounds that contradict our belief in a Good God who should treat us a bit better than this. Our theology might tell us that God doesn't cause this and yet we wonder why this is allowed. One person told me that God might be picking on me. She said, "God is teasing you." This was not my concept of God. Perhaps someday, I'll accept a theology of a teasing God, but at this point in my life, it just makes me shudder. Yet many times, our God is too small and we need to expand our theology and broaden our relationship with the Most Holy One and Wholly One.

Our struggle with health often triggers a struggle with faith. We might be fine about our belief in a loving God, but nevertheless, our faith in the future is shaken. We expect things to go one way, and they aren't going that way. Forcing life to go the way we want is like forcing a square peg into a round hole—it doesn't work. Yet we want to change things because our lives have become about our injury and not about freedom and liberation and love and goodness and life flowing like a beautiful river and all things working out for the good. We look to the future and just see more of the same—more of the same suffering, more of the same problems, more of the same despair, more of the same questions, more of the same life that seems to be riddled throughout with this illness that seems to affect everything in our lives. This weighs us down and weighs down our friends who don't like to see us struggle. They also grapple with theology—trying to understand why someone they love has to go through this.

It can seem so depressing, weighty, and miserable. And yet, some of the goodness that can come out of our illness may be an ability to see God in much bigger ways than we ever needed when we were well. When we become ill, we need to expand our theology and therefore, our relationship with God. None of this fluffy "hearts and flowers," "head in the clouds," "ain't life grand," kind of theology that leaves no room for the imperfections that permeate our lives. A theology that cannot deal with evil and flaws is not possible anymore. We're forced to change in some way, because our illness is like a thorn in our side that doesn't let go. It doesn't allow us to be oblivious.

We can, of course, sink into despair since this illness walks beside us all the time. Yet, our illness begs us to come to terms with some kind of meaning because the possibility of despair is always just over our shoulder. We're summoned to have a faith that recognizes the complexities and intricacies of human life and that is able, in the midst of difficulties, to still see God and trust God.

CHAPTER 3:

The Who What Why When And How

For I know the plans I have for you, declares the Lord, plans to prosper you and not to harm you, plans to give you hope and a future. Then you will call upon me and come and pray to me, and I will listen to you.
—Jeremiah 29:11–13

When journalists investigate news stories, they're filled with questions. They want to know what was going on, why it was going on, where it was going on, and when it was going on. They're taught in journalism school to ask very specific questions in order to get the whole story.

They're looking for the meaning of what is happening and they're looking for the "why."

Those of us who are ill are usually asking the same questions. We ask of the doctors, "What happened? Why did it happen? Who's at fault for it happening? How did it happen and how am I going to resolve it? What are my choices? How long is it going to last? What do I do about it?"

We also ask questions of God, "What are you doing? Why are you doing this to me? Why don't you stop it? When did I go so wrong that I had to be punished? Is it Karma? God's will? Or is it Fate or Destiny? Who's to blame? Is it me? Is it the person who hit me with the car? Is it the people around me who create an environment that is toxic? Is it me who had some long-term problem that I never noticed? How are You going to resolve this for me and how am I going to resolve this relationship with You? Are You really there? Are You the God who punishes or the God who saves? Are You a God who heals or are You a God that stands by and watches? Who are You to me in this process? And vice versa."

Questions. Questions. And more questions. The head spins and it gets exhausting! But they don't stop—at least not right away.

We might say to God, "I'm not sure who we are to each other now because our relationship was built on something else. You were my friend and now it seems You turned against me. You're the One that gave me happy days and now it seems that You are either giving me a bad time or allowing something or someone to give me a bad time. I thought You were my Heavenly Father who loved me and now I feel so unloved and so uncared-for. I thought You were my Guide, and yet I'm walking through the dark woods and I don't see a whole lot of light. I thought You were the One who protected me and I feel as if everything is coming at me and overwhelming me and I have no defenses."

We're besieged by unending, unyielding questions— like a hornet's nest that's been disturbed. Why now? Why me? Why this?

We think of our future relationship with God, especially if we feel our present relationship is unclear and tense. Like Job, we may decide it's perfectly alright to question God and argue with the Almighty. It may be we become bold and aggravating—like Job, our new model for insistent behavior that demands answers—or, at least, a response.

"What can we become if all our ways of thinking about You have to change? We even wonder if You are there. Where can You be in our life in the midst of our suffering?"

"How do we find You again? How do we see You differently and see You more honestly and see ourselves more honestly and see our relationship as having the potential to be full and caring and loving again?"

In the midst of this struggle, I decided not to turn my back on God. For me, there was no other place to be and no other place to stand—but on God's side. So I move more deeply into this relationship.

CHAPTER 4:

Becoming The Least Of These

If anyone wants to be first, he must be the very last,
and the servant of all.
—Mark 9:35

We've read many stories in the Bible of people being raised up and people moving from being "the least of these" to being "the most powerful" and "the most important." David was on the run, Saul was trying to kill him, and then David was raised up from Fugitive to King. Joseph was thrown into a pit and sold into slavery and spent years in prison, and then he became a leader of Egypt that saved Egypt and saved surrounding countries as well. Jesus advised when invited to a dinner or a wedding feast, take the least exalted place, and allow the host to raise you up. (Luke 14:8)

We might expect that the normal movement of our relationship with God is from being the least of these to being raised up and for God to exalt us, perhaps give us more power, perhaps give us more responsibility, perhaps give us more opportunities. We start life as being the smallest and we grow. We expect that same growth in our faith with our personal Walk with God.

But when we have a medical problem, we often move from being in a more exalted position to becoming one of the least of these. We go from being whole to being broken. We go from being healthy to being sick. We go from people who are included to being excluded, either because we're not able to do the activities we did before or because our friends have forgotten about us or because we're not around in the way we used to be. We have doctors' appointments instead of going to a dance. We have therapies to do and can't just gather at any time for discussions far into the evening or for long dinners or for a weekend away.

In the Good Samaritan story (Luke 10:25-37), we hear the story of three people who are the "least of these." The man who had fallen among thieves had gone from being whole to broken and battered and beaten and near death. He had become a man in great need of help. He was like dirt, as many people passed him by, not caring, not responding.

The story is also about the thief who beat him. The thief is worthless. Thieves are "the least of these" in our society. Thieves live on the very fringes of society and much of their time is spent doing harm to others. Of what benefit are they to society? They're not improving society. They're not adding to people's comfort levels. They're not helping other people. They're not adding to the economy because they, undoubtedly, are not paying taxes on what they've stolen. They seem to be a remnant of society, a sideline. They're not important, or powerful, or influential, except for the problems they cause us. They're "the least of these." "Hang 'em high," we say, "Let them rot in prison." "Any punishment they get, they deserve."

The Samaritan who saved the near-dying man was also one of the least of these. Samaritans were shunned by the Jews. Travelers would try to bypass the town of Samaria. Jews didn't speak to Samaritans because they were not accepted as suitably religious. They were not kosher; they were not part of the Inner Circle.

Jesus told the story of The Good Samaritan to Jews. This would be similar to telling a Ku Klux Klan member about a black man who was a good model of humanity. At the end of the story of the Good Samaritan, when the Samaritan takes care of the man who had fallen among thieves, Jesus says, "Go and do likewise." (Luke 10)

Jesus recognized the Samaritan as the good neighbor. He told his listeners to do what the Samaritan did: to care for the hurt, the rejected, the forsaken.

But there is another layer of meaning that is interpreted by the theologian Karl Barth, which I find very meaningful, particularly in the midst of my own physical problems. Barth said, "Go and do likewise and be in need." Barth recognized that all of us are in need much like the man who has fallen among thieves. Yes, all of us—the rich, poor, educated, illiterate, the insiders or outsiders—we all stand in need. We are vulnerable. We are fragile. We are broken and need somebody who can come along and help make us whole. For some, this is hard to swallow—our humanness, our imperfection.

Many people intensely dislike being in need. We're taught to be independent and self-sufficient and to be our own person and not to have to rely on other people who might be unreliable. Yet there is a recognition in this story that the care the Good Samaritan gives, is the care that we all need.

I find it very helpful to recognize my human condition as being one of the least of these in need of being rescued. The man among thieves was probably not capable of reaching out to anyone or even moaning or crying for help. The situation demanded somebody notice him, and do something.

Sometimes when we're the least of these, we recognize we don't have the capability to call for help. Nor do we see anybody around us who would want to give us help. Certainly, if the man among thieves had looked up and been able to choose his savior, he would have chosen the Priest or the Levite and not the Samaritan.

But when we're in need, we might be surprised at the people who become the instruments of God. Perhaps our help comes from the nurse's aide who recently arrived from Honduras who has little education and speaks broken English, and yet she is the one who gives a smile and encouragement and the courage to carry on. Maybe it's your neighbor who you have rarely talked to because you don't think you have anything in common. And yet, this is the person who brings you food and that is better medicine for you than the prescription drugs.

When my sister, who had ALS, was in her final months, a black nurse assistant from Jamaica moved into their home. She became like a sister to my sister despite their different backgrounds. I thought the doctor who was a specialist would have been her great helper. But it was Dawn who was her angel. There was something so beautiful about their relationship and Dawn's devotion to my sister for these last six months. My sister insisted Dawn sit with our family at her funeral and we were all happy to have her as one of us.

We're often surprised by who is not acting as the instrument of God. I have gone to doctors who have nothing to offer me and didn't have a real concern about my condition. I had a doctor walk out of the room when I told him that I didn't want a Botox shot. He was terribly dismissive and even rude.

I have found help and concern and care from people whom ordinarily I would not expect. Many people I've met are wise and insightful, including other patients who might even be more broken than I am. Many of my screenwriting students and clients have had compassion and sometimes have made recommendations. We find when we're one of the least of these, we learn to open our hearts to help from whatever corner it comes from.

When we're healthy and doing our normal work, we have often figured out who the people are that can be helpful to us and who are not. Perhaps unconsciously, we rank people according to what they can do for us or how powerful they are. Most of the time, the people who seem to be more powerful and at a higher ranking are the ones we look to for help to raise us up. But when we're in need, we might suddenly recognize that it is not the powerful who make a difference in our lives, but the ones who have compassion and care. We change our value system because we learn that God can work through anyone. Perhaps some of us who have an expectation about who will help us might be surprised that the helper could be a thief (like the thief on the Cross) or could be our supposed enemy, the Samaritan.

CHAPTER 5:

Where Do We Stand?

Here I stand; I cannot do otherwise. So help me God!
—Martin Luther

There is a verse in the Bible where Jesus asks the disciples whether they want to leave Him. Simon Peter answered, "Lord, to whom shall we go?" (John 6:68) Peter chose to stand with Jesus.

It is easy when we're ill to stand on the side of despair. There is so much that is overwhelming and taxing to us. We can easily stand on the side of a shadowy life where we can feel pushed off of our center. We try to steady ourselves and yet we find ourselves in a disturbing place where we don't feel peace or in harmony with life. But in spite of illness, there is only one place to stand.

Sometimes it's difficult to find God when we're in the midst of our illness. God doesn't instill in us the sense of peace that we wish for. God doesn't work miracles for us on command—at least not at the moment. God doesn't do what we want Him to do. It's easy to just roll with the punches and eventually be punched down. But where can we stand? It seems as if there's only one place to stand, even when we don't understand. We can continue to believe that somewhere at the center of life, there is something that is good. There is no other place for us to be but to take our stand with the belief that, in spite of everything, goodness and kindness and love absolutely have to prevail, and are able to prevail in the midst of all of our problems.

CHAPTER 6:

Shunning The Shadowy Dark Force

In the Devil's pack...
it is only the cards of love which are missing...
—Dag Hammarskjold

In the early stages of my suffering, one of my friends said to me, "You are under attack." She said that illness really works against the perfection of what it means to be human. Illness is not of God. It must be resisted. God wants us to be healthy and God wants us to be the best human beings we can be—physically, mentally, psychologically, and spiritually. Anything that works against the sense of perfection and wholeness is an enemy.

Some might say that anything not Of the Light comes from the will of the devil, sometimes called Satan, or sometimes called the Dark Side of Life. Illness can bring us down into despair, depression, anger, and resignation. Certainly all of these things are harmful to us and are to be resisted.

There have been times during my illness when I felt there was a shadowy dark side that was actually trying to pull me away from God. The illness led me to a dark place that made it easier for me to question my faith, to question my belief in God, to question the nature of God. During that time, when I was even hazy about God, I found the best thing to do was to say to the Dark Force, "I'm not yours. You don't get me." There were times I visualized a circle around me as if this circle embraced me and put me on the side of God. There were times that I felt that I didn't need to know a whole lot about the nature of God; I had to recognize that I stood on God's side, whether or not I saw God clearly.

There were other times that I visualized Jesus as a brother and friend standing next to me and helping me. Sometimes I imagined Jesus saying to the Dark Force, "She isn't yours, she's mine. You don't get her!" For several months, every time I felt the Dark Force, I continued to repeat: "I'm not yours. You don't get me."

One evening I saw the Dark Force out of the corner of my eye slinking away. There was something about this constant affirmation of where I stood that had a certain power. I didn't need to know everything about God, but I did know if I had to choose where I stood, I had to stand on the side of goodness and loving kindness, and a belief that wholeness is possible. I stand by the Power of the Holy Spirit.

An acquaintance of mine who has dystonia told me she often thought God would say, "She is mine and did nothing to bring this on herself so let her be!"

We fight that shadow and we continue to resist the Darkness. We belong wholly on the side of Light —on the side of God.

CHAPTER 7:

Reviewing Our Situation

Healing is a matter of time, but it is sometimes also a matter of opportunity.
—Hippocrates

Most illnesses or injuries fall into one of four categories: for some, the injury needs to heal and the doctors have worked with enough of these types of injuries so they can tell the patient how long it will take and what is needed in order to heal. If someone has a broken arm, the doctor might say, "Your arm is broken and, if you do the following exercises and you don't hurt it again, and if you are very careful, in three months' time you'll be as good as new. Your arm will have healed and you'll have full mobility and you'll be back to normal." The doctors have seen enough patients with this injury that they can be quite clear about what is needed. It is up to the patient to do the therapies to strengthen that area so they can meet the timeline that the doctor has predicted. If they do the therapies, the patient can be reasonably sure about how it will go. The patient still has to cope with immobility, therapy, and pain for a period of time. They disrupt their lifestyle and still might feel frustration and impatience and concern, but they have a future that will be back to normal.

There are other injuries that are not going to get better and the patient has to learn to deal with being maimed, crippled, or diminished by the injury. A soldier who has a leg blown off as a result of stepping on a mine or being shot is not going to re-grow the leg. Unless there's a miracle, the soldier's life is going to be a life without a leg, and the challenge is to learn to deal with it. There can be some healing and rehabilitation and the doctor might say, "If you do the following therapies you have a reasonably good chance of getting a prosthetic device and having some mobility. This might take three to six months or a year before you're able to be fully rehabilitated, but you can still have a good life, even though it's a life without a leg."

There are some illnesses where the patient will be in a long decline. Someone who is advanced in age, or who has a terminal illness may know they won't get better, and their time on Earth is limited.

My sister knew she would die of ALS within two to three years. She once said, "Unlike others, I know how I will die." I asked her if she had any intuition about when it would happen and she responded, "It's the Lord's timing." In those last years, we all experienced joy, closeness, laughter, and humor. By observing my sister, I realized that it is possible to die a Good Death, and to be an inspiration to others in the process.

There are other injuries where the doctor doesn't know how it's going to go and whether full recovery is possible and whether life will be different and how long will it take for something to be changed, if it can be changed. This is my case with dystonia. Both of my doctors think there is a possibility I will recover completely. Each of them has had a patient who has completely recovered. Each of them knows of others who have recovered. There are cases of recovery for dystonia mentioned online, although there is no way to contact these people to know if these cases are true. The doctors are not specific about how this will go, how long it will take, and whether this is something I need to adjust to and surrender to for the rest of my life or whether there is a possibility of full recovery. The doctors don't give me a timeline for a cure. Another doctor said dystonia is not curable. Period.

Although it seems odd, my experience with cancer has been much easier. I have at least ten friends and relatives who have gone through what I have gone through, and have survived for many, many years. At this point in cancer research, doctors know the percentages of possibilities for survival. There is plenty of information and a great deal of support for cancer patients and almost none for those with dystonia.

Each injury or illness demands something different from the patient. All of them demand a type of surrender to the process that is going on, a tremendous amount of courage, an astronomical amount of fortitude and perseverance and commitment, and a constant fighting against the despair that can so easily set in. We fight this on a daily basis. I mentioned to Dr. Henry one day that I was feeling very discouraged. Her response was immediate and strong and assertive: "Don't go there. It's not good for your brain and it's not good for your healing." I often have remembered her words because that dark side of our nature, sometimes called The Shadow, reminds us of our vulnerabilities. The Shadow is a term used by Dr. Carl Jung and other psychotherapists because we so seldom are consciously aware of it, yet it holds all the frustrations and rage we usually suppress in order to get along in relatively normal ways. Even though our illness is not our normal self, and though it seems like falling into the dark side might be the only way, it is our job to fight this Shadow with every fiber of our being, with every cell in our bodies, with every thought that we can. It is clear that we must not let despair take over.

I don't know how people fight this without some kind of a spiritual life. We might define this in different ways, whether we believe it's the Breath of God that inhabits us or whether we experience The Light Within or whether we have a feeling that Jesus is by our side or that the Holy Spirit works through us and moves us and guides us into a fuller, deeper life. Many of us would agree that there is a Spiritual Essence that is friendly to us, gracious to us, strengthens us, and comforts us, and makes it possible to go on. It is a Spirit we can call on at all times.

Many years ago Leonard Bernstein, the renowned composer and conductor, composed a long piece of music that is called "Mass." In that music there is a lovely song that said, "When my heart is lonely and everything I have is gone, I will face regret, all my days and yet, I will still go on."

Endurance is not often listed as one of the greatest virtues, but it's a virtue those of us who are ill desperately need. Although I want God to be the One Who Heals, I have been most amazed at experiencing God as the One who strengthens me, upholds me, and makes it possible for me to endure.

Somehow we keep going. That's a miracle.

PART TWO:

The Journey of Faith, Dialogue, and Try

CHAPTER 8:

Standing Within Job's Circle

Have you not put a hedge around [Job]
and his household and everything he has?
—Job 1:9

One of the books in the Bible that might speak specifically to our condition is the book of *Job*. Everything fell upon him—mental and physical anguish, loss of people close to him, a tremendous sickness, and the uncertainty and struggle that comes because friends did not understand him. In the book of *Job*, God puts a hedge or circle around Job and lets Satan know how far he can go with the punishment of Job. God says Satan can take almost everything, but he must spare his life.

When we're ill, it might seem as if everything is taken away from us: our mobility, our flexibility, our ability to go out into the world and to do fun things and to play and laugh and dance and be free. However, rarely is everything taken away from us. A circle is drawn around us and, in most cases, we don't lose as much as Job lost. Often there are many parts of our lives that are protected and that are actually blessed in the midst of illness. It may be that our families stand strongly with us. A spouse might be unwavering in his or her support. We might have friends who stand within that circle with us. They're not separated from us as a result of illness, but in many cases, actually become closer to us.

Our work, in one way or another, might be protected. It may be, in spite of our illness, we're able to do our work, continue with our careers, and we might even find new skills and new opportunities as a result. Many of us have illnesses where we don't lose our homes and are able to enjoy the comfort of a place that nurtures us. In my case, I had a horse and wondered if I needed to stop riding, but all my doctors said that riding was very good for me and very therapeutic. My horse was protected and remained within the circle of blessings. Probably in almost all of our cases, there is something good that remains. God has put a circle around it and said, "You may not take this away even though this person is ill and even though this person is struggling."

Job's friends, like many friends, tried to analyze why this terrible thing happened to him, placing some of the blame on Job, saying he wasn't righteous enough. It is part of the "If Only" thinking and part of a Blame Theology. There has to be a reason. It's obviously your fault.

Job continually felt their reasoning was not correct. Like them, Job was asking the question, "Why? Why is this happening to me?" When the Voice of God finally came to Job, He did not answer the question of "Why?" Instead,

God said, "Where were you when I created the world?" The answer, logically, makes no sense. It's a non sequitur. It is not the answer to the question. God is really saying, "The answer doesn't lie with reason and logic. The answer lies with some experience of God and some recognition of The Mystery." In that moment, Job had an encounter with God that was far more important than getting the answer he sought.

I would guess that for most of us there are some experiences that help us touch the divine and the sacred. It might be an experience of grace. It might be an experience of being taken care of, in spite of everything. It might be an experience of love in the midst of our troubles. It might be an experience of people reaching out to us in a way that gives us comfort. It might be an experience of the deep kindness that we can get from a spouse, from relatives, from friends. It is not all neat. It is not all clear. The meaning doesn't come from pure logic.

Job then answered God by saying, "Before, I knew you only by hearsay but now, having seen you with my own eyes ... I repent." (Job 42:5–6) (New Jerusalem Bible)

We move from trying to figure it all out to affirming the Mystery. The real question might be, "How do I keep a sense of the Presence of the Divine in the midst of this? How do I allow God to infiltrate my life when my illness feels as if it is keeping God out? How do I learn to recognize that His Living Presence is at the center of life, and that the center of life cannot be moved, even as a result of my illness? How do I recognize that nothing truly can keep me from the love of God?"

CHAPTER 9.

Refusing To Curse God

*God has a use for you, even though what He asks doesn't
happen to suit you at the moment.*
—Dag Hammarskjod

Our concept of God is tested when we're ill. When Job
had troubles thrust upon him, his wife said, "Curse God
and die." He was tempted and challenged to see God as
being mean-spirited. It seemed like the only response—to
curse God as a result of these terrible trials and tribulations. But Job refused. In spite of all the problems, he kept
believing and having faith that there was some meaning in
this and that God had not deserted him.

When I was a seminary student, I directed a reader's
theater production of the book of *Job*. As I researched the
book and the individual verses within the book, I came
to the conclusion that his friends were standing between
him and God, and that he was not able to see God clearly, because the confusion of the disease and the logic and

analysis of his friends were getting in the way.

When I staged this production, I put an altar in the middle as if that were where God was located. I had the friends continually stand between Job and the altar. As Job began to see God more clearly, he began to see the omnipresence of God and realized he couldn't locate God in one place. God became a God of all spaces by the end of the production and the friends could no longer keep Job from God.

In truth, no one can really stand between us and God, although it seems as if many people and many things do. It seems as if the bad wishes and often the good wishes of our friends and the bad and good intentions of others can get in the way. It seems as if our physical disabilities get in the way between us and God. The doctors with their good advice, but sometimes bad advice, can get in the way since we see them as healers and then we discover that they're simply educated people trying to hopefully help— but they're not little gods. People who don't understand can get in the way. Relatives and friends who think there's something wrong with us for not getting better can get in the way. But in truth, the circle that puts us and God within the circle is not a circle that can be broken unless we allow it to. The urge to curse God and to see God as the one who has brought this pain upon us can get in our way, but it doesn't need to. Job refused to curse God in spite of everything that seemed to say cursing God was appropriate.

There are many temptations throughout our illness and this may be the greatest—to put the blame on God, to see God as mean-spirited and nasty and desiring bad things for us. Although I'm not a person who generally uses profanities or vulgarities, I have more than once screamed, "dammit!" in my extreme frustration. I don't think I have cursed God, but I have cursed my situation.

I have been angry at God, even enraged. More than once I have told God, "I don't want to talk to you right now." I have looked at the chair where I do my morning meditations and said, "I'm not sitting there today. I'm so angry I don't think you're on my side." Sometimes I've scolded God for not doing His part. Bad girl!

The temptation is there—to curse God and to die. This death might not just be a physical death, but a temptation to allow a spiritual death to happen. We're tempted to believe we can get along without God who seems to be so mean to us. We're challenged to refuse this temptation.

CHAPTER 10:

The Try

Be strong . . . and work. For I am with you.
—Haggai 2:4

My avocation for many years was horseback riding. When entering the world of horses in my 40s, I learned that horses are often judged by the extent to which the horse has "Try." In cowboy language, the word "try" is sometimes used as a noun, not a verb. Sometimes a cowboy will say, "The horse doesn't have *try*." Or "the horse has *try*—I think we should buy that horse!" When buying a horse, one looks for the willingness, for the try. Although simply trying doesn't always gain extra points in the show ring, once in a while it does because the willingness of the horse convinces the judge. If the horse hasn't tried, if he isn't willing, and he puts his ears back, swishes his tail, and throws his head, it is no longer a pretty sight and the unwillingness is clear to everybody.

One of the qualities that is asked of us by our doctors is

to be a person with *try*. The doctors want us to be willing to have faith in the therapies, to keep our appointments, to believe in the possibility of improvement, and even the possibility of a full recovery. We might say that the model patient has *try*. Several doctors have told me that there are so many patients that don't try and that don't do their therapies and don't follow through. When they do, a patient will often say to the doctor, "What do you know? It really worked!" In the horse world, sometimes *try* is just as good as actually having done it. In the world of patients, as well as in the world of horses, *try* really counts.

Many times, when taking a riding lesson, I'd been working on a particular maneuver with my horse. Sometimes my trainer would say, "Good! He tried to do what you asked him to do. He didn't get it this time but he will. Give him a pat. Let him relax and feel good for a moment." His *try* is considered *as if* he had done the maneuver correctly.

I think that this is what is often demanded of us—to become people who have try. Some of us are already those kind of people and know how to do that—others of us learn during the process. We're asked to try *as if* we'll get better. Trying is an act of Faith. It believes in Hope and a Future. We continue to try to be people with try.

CHAPTER 11:

Creating The Team

Carry each other's burdens, and in this way you will
fulfill the law of Christ.
—Galatians 6:2

It seems like such a simple and obvious thing —to call on our spiritual community during a time of need. But it's so easy to forget to do this. Think about who gives you comfort, insight, wisdom, helps you adjust your attitude when necessary, encourages you, gives you courage, and helps you through.

At the beginning of an illness, we can feel very alone and without comfort or help, wondering whether there is anyone who has ever been here before and whether there's anyone who can be of help to us. It is true that there are people in our lives who don't give us spiritual sustenance and instead can add to our burden. There are people who can make us feel guilty or at fault for whatever problems we're encountering. There are people who demand we do what we're incapable of doing —such as exercising more, getting out rather than being isolated, praying more, looking at ourselves to see who's at fault.

But there are other people we can bring into our lives, who really do work as a conduit for the love of God. They're God's hands reaching out to us at times when we need a physical and concrete presence. When we're in those darkest moments, that's when we need to have our spiritual team.

Sometimes I have very consciously assembled my team. I've asked specific people if they're willing to help, recognizing that each one of them offers me something just a little bit different.

One of the people on my team loves to pray and she fervently begs and pleads and asks God to reach out to me and to help me feel God's love. One time, she asked God to give me a sign of His guidance. Then something interesting happened shortly after her prayer. I needed to buy some boxes in order to pack up our Christmas decorations. I looked in the Yellow Pages for the box stores nearby. None of them was very near, but I called one and he gave me an address and I set out to go the 20 minutes out of my way to pick up some boxes. As I drove, I got more and more frustrated because I couldn't find this address and I was running out of time. I intended to get the boxes and then go to a movie, which is something I occasionally desperately needed to do. Finally, I decided to head straight for the movie and deal with the boxes later. As I prepared to get on the freeway to get to the movie theater exit, the freeway was backed up by about 20 cars. I have never seen a freeway backed up like this in Colorado Springs (it's common in LA) and I was surprised, but decided I would take one of the side streets. I wasn't sure where to make my turn as I didn't know this area well, but I saw a street that I recognized and turned on Nevada to go to downtown Colorado Springs. As I was driving, on the corner was a store with big letters that announced, "The Box Store." Ah! A sign?

Yes, definitely a sign! It was a store I had not seen advertised in the Yellow Pages but there it was.

Now how do we interpret this? Coincidence? A metaphor? A personal God guiding and directing? As a Christian, I'm trying to see the Hand of God more often and to sense that Presence which calms me and comforts me. I pulled in and the salesperson was a great help in choosing exactly the right boxes for our Christmas decorations. As I left the store, I thought of the metaphor of the circuitous route. I felt as if there was guidance. I recognized that we often take a circuitous route and have blockages and obstacles and doors that are closed and fences that force us into a different direction and yet, there I was driving to my destination. I couldn't help but remember how Susan had fervently prayed that I would have a sign of God's love and guidance. And I recognized the metaphor of my journey. I also got to the movie on time!

I have some people on my spiritual team who seem to know all the right verses in the Bible to give me comfort. I have other people on my spiritual team who have read a great deal of spiritual literature and have quotes to give me that add to the meaning of this darkness. I have some people on my team who are extremely compassionate and sit with me or talk to me or have a silent, quiet, centered presence. I have some who are incredibly wise and put my situation into perspective. I have a wonderful spiritual director who is a Benedictine nun who helps me to see the hand of God. She encourages me, supports me in my search, and affirms my direction. At times when I feel as if I'm not doing well spiritually at all, she helps me to see that I'm following a glimmer of light and even affirms the fact that I have not given up the search.

I have two doctors on my team who are both spiritual. One of my doctors, Dr. Michaele Sparaco-Posey from Colorado Springs, gives me courage. I haven't always figured out exactly how she does that because it's more than just encouragement. I just know that after I talk to her, I feel my courage is reborn and I'm able to go on and feel strength and fortitude.

My doctor in Houston, Dr. Gail Henry, is one of the leaders and acknowledged experts on *cervical dystonia.* She gives me wisdom, clarity, and insight -- all with great kindness and sensitivity -- which puts things into perspective. I know she's always on my side, directing me.

Both doctors are very good at what they do but give me far more than their medical skills. Sometimes I think of Dr. Henry as "Sophia," my wisdom and Dr. Sparaco-Posey as "Earth Mother." I need them both.

The circle around us is a protective circle. The team is not just a matter of people who can heal us or people who can help improve our condition but also a spiritual team.

A spouse and relatives and immediate family can also

be a great source of comfort if we love them and they love us. It is easy not to share our struggles with those very close to us. But they can be the core of our support and remind us of our strong roots.

This is a time to affirm our spiritual community such as our church or synagogue or spiritual friends. I have been tremendously sustained by my Quaker community. I confronted my Quaker community at one of my darkest times because I didn't think or feel that they understood my plight or my struggle. Their response was heartfelt. They understood. This often happens because most people don't see that there's anything wrong with me and, as a result, it's easy for them to believe there's no struggle.

Gathering our community and also leaning on them when necessary is our privilege, especially with those people who claim to be spiritual. I think we have the right to ask them if they're willing to step up to the plate and to be there for us. To some extent, our spiritual life gives us permission to ask them to stand with us if they're able. When I feel hesitant to ask, I often tell myself, "The Bible tells me we're supposed to help each other. Go ahead. Ask!" I have discovered that there are many people who would like to help if only they knew how to help. It is up to us to call them and to embrace the help that they're able to give us.

Catholics also have their saints who are part of their spiritual community. Although I'm not Catholic, I have at times drawn on the wisdom of the many Catholic saints, with some of my favorites being St. Theresa of Avila, St. Luke the physician, St. Therese of Lisieux, and St. Frances of Assisi.

Our spiritual community also can include those who write books that speak to our condition.

For those of us who are Christian, we call on the Trinity —the Holy Spirit who fills us and is a Comforter and Guide; God the Holy One, the Heavenly Father (who some also think of as the Heavenly Mother,) God the Sustainer, God our help in time of trouble; Jesus the Healer, The Suffering Servant and the Beloved.

As I started to look for help in all directions, I had a dream in which God was a sea captain. We were on a very large passenger ship where I was the only other person on that ship. God pointed out to me that there were many, many rooms on the ship and many hallways. I could explore as I wanted. We were in the middle of a great sea, and I had no idea how one would navigate a sea where there were no markers and no sign of land. As I talked to God, I saw God as my Navigator, my Sea Captain, my Guide, the One who knows what He's doing and where we're going, the One in whom I should put my trust, the One who cares about me personally.

After awakening, I continued to have a conversation with God —a kind of dialogue. I started asking questions, and I sensed answers. The dream occurred about 4:00 in the morning and I decided to just keep talking to God as long as I felt I was getting wise answers. My husband occasionally came up to check on me, and I just said, "I'm talking to God and I'm not giving up until this conversation is finished." God and I talked until 9:00 a.m. —five hours. The dream gave me a sense of comfort and a sense that I was in good hands.

At various times, I began to experience Jesus as my Brother and my Friend and my Helper. Before that, I had seen Jesus as the healer and had constantly been calling on Him to heal me. Now I began to also see Jesus as the Suffering Servant entering into the human condition and being willing to say "yes" to all the darkness.

At other times, I began to feel the sense of the Holy Spirit as a breath. It was fresh. It was within me. It was a sweet presence.

I then began to experience Wisdom who helped me perceive and have insights about this condition. "Wisdom" in Greek is the word, "Sophia." In the Bible, wisdom is personified. If you read Proverbs 8, you'll read about Wisdom being a co-creator and a master craftsperson with God in the creation of the world. She is also discussed in the Psalms, in some sections of St. Paul's writing, and also in the *Apocrypha*, which is in the Catholic Bible but not in the Protestant Bible.

King Solomon was considered the wisest ruler in the Hebrew Scriptures. He sought Wisdom above all else and considered Wisdom more precious than rubies or any other precious gem. There is something wonderful about calling on Wisdom in all of our difficulties. There are a number of verses that tell us that Wisdom is there waiting at our back door on the doorstep for us to come and talk to her. There are other verses that say that God loves the person who seeks Wisdom (Proverbs 3, 4, 8, and *The Book of Wisdom* and *Ecclesiasticus* from the *Apocrypha* are all about Wisdom).

In our illness, there are so many times that we need to

call on Wisdom. We need Wisdom to select the right doctors. We need Wisdom to do research about our illness. We need Wisdom to know when we're overwhelmed and when it's time to call on other people to come to our aid. We need Wisdom to know what therapies to follow and when someone is suggesting something that really isn't right for us or good for us. We get suggestions from many, many people and we need the wisdom to know what is worth following, what is overwhelming, and what is silly advice. We need Wisdom to make the right decisions and to make clear choices in the midst of all the chaos that surrounds illness.

There's something beautiful when we realize the wisdom that we need is here for us. I have felt her guidance at times in terms of how to react or what to do next or how to even be more in touch with my body and what my body was telling me about what worked and didn't work. I call on her as a feminine nurturing presence that helps get me through, day by day.

Our spiritual community can be vast. We might feel that we're on our own in the midst of our struggles. We are not. In spite of the fact that probably no one on earth can really reach out and make everything better, there are many people that can give us light and comfort.

And of course, there are so many dimensions of God that speak to our condition. We never walk alone and God promises never to leave us alone.

CHAPTER 12:

Creator–Judge–Restorer

The Redeemer is also The Creator. He, the One that Judgeth, is also He The One that restoreth all things
—Karl Barth

What were we created to be? What are we supposed to become during our lives? What qualities are intrinsic to us as human beings and what flaws and imperfections seep into us over the years? Who are we when we're ill? And who are we when we're well?

One image of God that we might think about is the image of God the Creator. Not just the Creator of Heaven and Earth but the Creator of us. According to the Creation stories, God gave us breath. God gave us the spark. The New Testament talks about God giving us the Holy Spirit as a comforter and a counselor. The Spirit in the Hebrew Scriptures is sometimes described as a wind.

If we think of how we were created, it seems as if the Spirit pulls us toward Goodness, Peace, and Joy. We were created to live in harmony in the garden with the animals and each other and walk easily with God. But something went wrong and, whether we call that something disobedience, or turning our backs on God, or stepping away into pride or arrogance or wanting too much control or power —this entrenched harmony was turned into something that became broken and that takes the form of angst, warfare, disease, anger, resistance, and anxiety.

Eventually, these imperfections begin to have an effect on us. Sometimes the effect is mental or psychological or physical. Sometimes that effect comes from things that we do to ourselves and other times it comes because we're out of relationship with others or others are out of relationship with us. Sometimes our problems result from the problems of others.

We can keep our eyes on what we believe our creation was meant to be and where things went wrong. We might think of this mythologically, thinking of our ideal places when things all seemed to be working well within our bodies and within our relationships. There are some who interpret the Garden of Eden as this place that we hold inside of ourselves as "how it was supposed to be." Some might think, "When was my life at its happiest?" Or "When did I feel the most whole and in what ways has that changed?" We can meditate on where the Garden of Eden was for us, and what was Fallen as we moved out of how we were created to be.

God the Judge is an image that can be found throughout the Judeo-Christian religion and undoubtedly in many others. We sometimes think of the term "judge" as a punitive and vengeful word and we might believe that our illness is a punishment. But what if God is defined as the "fair judge" and the "just judge" rather than the "punitive judge?" We often feel judgment within us. Whether we feel our bodies or our minds are judging us or whether we think God is judging us, we sometimes feel a sense of blame for our particular illnesses. Sometimes the illness seems to be a direct result of a judgment that our bodies have made. For instance, we now know that smoking causes lung cancer. It doesn't cause lung cancer for everybody, but it's certainly responsible for many, many cases. If somebody has been smoking for years and gets lung cancer, they might say, "This illness is a judgment on me," or "My body is judging me." They might judge themselves, saying, "This was not a good idea to constantly put toxins into my body and eventually this became very destructive to my health."

If somebody drinks a lot and then gets sick or has a car accident because they were drunk, they might recognize this as a judgment on themselves. There are certainly many diseases that can be tracked directly to living out of harmony. And many of us struggle with trying to understand what is the cause of our illness. Are we overeating? Are we working too hard and causing too much stress on ourselves? Are we not exercising and not keeping our bodies tuned? Are we letting things eat away at us mentally? Are we around constant irritation or negative thoughts or anger that begins to have an effect on us? To what extent is our illness a consequence of our own actions?

Sometimes something happens to us and we wonder

if God is judging us for something we don't even know we did. Other times, we see the innocent suffering. How many children get hurt or sick through no fault of their own?

One time, someone said to me, "This isn't God's fault. You don't have dystonia or cancer because God gave it to you." In the case of dystonia, I was the victim of somebody else's poor judgment. The person who drove the car that caused my medical problem didn't understand that red means *stop* and green means *go*.

Some medical professionals say that we will all get cancer if we live long enough. Some of us get it earlier because of family history or environmental problems, but it still isn't God's fault. There is a Hungarian proverb that says, "Adam ate the apple and our teeth still ache." If in doubt, we can always blame Adam.

Illness is often the time for us to rethink our lives and to change our lives. Maybe it means we slow up. Or, we don't work as much. Maybe we give up something detrimental to our health. Times of rehabilitation often give us an opportunity to reflect and rethink and perhaps even put a judgment on ourselves that tells us, "Forgive me for the bad choices I made in the past. I want to change this." We might tell God, "Just get me better. Please don't put another trip on me because I already have enough to deal with." It's natural for us to try to figure out the meaning and the blame.

But how do we continue to do better? God is the Restorer, the most Holy Spirit who works with us and through us to bring us back to the harmony for which we were created. God can work with broken pieces. That doesn't mean we'll get back to exactly where we were before. God is creative, and our new creation through God might not be what we expect.

We so often think of "restoration" as bringing it back to where we were before and polishing us up a bit to make us glow even brighter. And that often is true—we regain the life we had and it's an ever better life. Certainly Job regained his life, but with more insight and even more prosperity. But sometimes it doesn't go that way.

One of my clients is blind, totally blind, as a result of an accident. As he rehabilitated, he found that many times doctors turned to him because he had been through 23 surgeries on his face and, although they were not able to save his sight, they were able to save him. The doctors have learned much from the operations and from his feedback and from whom he has become. He gives speeches around the country. He's done a short film and has written a book about his experiences. He said to me that what has happened to him, in the long run, has been very good. In fact, if he had the chance to have the blindness removed (which would mean having all the good he's done removed) he said he would not take that opportunity. He has been restored to a new being and a new creation. He says with God's help, he has made good come out of this.

So restoration may not include complete healing, but it still can involve a new creation.

We're brought into new directions. That which was out of harmony in the past has been rehabilitated. *God maketh all things new* and our illnesses might actually be part of a new beginning if we're willing to be clay in the hands of the Potter, if we're willing to allow The Holy Spirit to move us into New Beings.

CHAPTER 13:

Wall Talks and Garden Walks

"Jesus our brother, kind and good."
—Traditional English song

There is a technique often used for relaxation or healing called Active Imagination. This is what I was doing when I imagined God as the sea captain and let the scene unfold. Often this is done where you imagine yourself in an ideal setting, whether by a mountain stream or a placid lake or a beautiful ocean with the surf coming in. As you sit in this scene, often you will start breathing more slowly and you will feel more relaxed. Sometimes you get insights about your condition or the scene unfolds and takes you somewhere. Sometimes you just feel calm in the midst of the chaos that comes with illness. Sometimes you add a person to the scene who might have wisdom to help you.

This could be a religious figure such as Jesus or Buddha or Mohammed or a saint, or it could be a person that has gone through something similar to what you're experiencing. It is said that sometimes First Ladies imagine talking to Eleanor Roosevelt, asking for wisdom about how to handle their role.

In the early stages of dystonia, I was told not to use Active Imagination because these images actually triggered the turning of my neck. Supposedly, my imaginative right cortex is overly active. The right cortex is the source of visual images so awakening those images for me makes the muscles in my neck even more reactive. My doctor has always been very respectful of my very active imagination, but for some period of time, suggested I not work with these images.

Then as I began to improve, the doctor led me through an Active Imagination exercise where I was to simply be aware of my breathing and nothing else. Then I was to imagine counting from 1 to 5 and after each number, simply say, "Deep relax," so that I continue to relax more and more as I move into the exercise. Then, I was to imagine going into an elevator and moving from floor A to B to C to D, becoming more and more relaxed at each floor. I would get out of the elevator and identify my pain level and imagine a lever taking me from pain level four to three to two to one and then zero. Then I would get back into the elevator and move up to Level A and then count from five down to one and at number one, my eyes would open.

As I was doing this exercise morning after morning, I

noticed when I came out of the elevator on Level D that there was something across the road from me. It was sort of blurry trees.

One day as I was doing this exercise, I decided to see what was across the road and I went over and noticed a short, pink adobe wall with an arch that led into a garden. I walked through the arch, wondering what was in there. There was Jesus waiting for me. (Maybe you've noticed that we all recognize Him!) How interesting! I think I'll stick around a bit.

A few months before this, when I was desperately seeking some wisdom on situations ranging from business challenges to medical challenges, I would occasionally imagine sitting on a low wall with Jesus and asking for insight. I would notice that the wall was in the Mount of Olives because there were olive trees and it was similar to what I remembered when I was in Jerusalem some years ago. I called them Wall Talks since we always sat on the wall. I would feel very calm as we talked.

This situation was a little different. I hadn't asked for Jesus to be there as I did in the wall talks. He was just there. I started to always go to the garden when I got out of the elevator. I noticed as I took these garden walks every morning, that we did very little talking. Jesus would take me around and draw my attention to my environment. As a result of my garden walks, just as I felt with my wall talks, I began to get insight and peace.

One time we just sat and listened to the birds. Another time, He took me toward the back of the garden where there was a children's playground. He introduced me to a little Muslim girl who he said was very special to Him. When I think of it now, she reminded me of the young Malala, who is the Pakistani girl that won the Nobel Peace Prize.

Sometimes, we simply went into a forest and He drew my awareness to the beauty of the trees. Once, we were by Lake Galilee. My sister was on a chair by the sea playing her flute with guitarist, Christopher Parkening. One time we walked through a field of lavender. I never knew what would develop when I walked into the garden, but I learned to trust that Jesus was always waiting for me. In Active Imagination, nothing is forced and you allow the images to evolve as they naturally develop. This means that you don't know what's going to happen, you have no expectations, and you don't even know who might appear.

As the walks and talks continued, we started to have healing sessions. I would imagine Jesus putting his hands on my neck where these muscles were in spasm. I would then put my hands on my neck and tenderly massage where I felt I was directed. I noticed as the session went on, that my neck became more still and I was able to hold my head more centered without much turning or straining.

When I was in seminary, I participated in the Spiritual Exercises of St. Ignatius. St. Ignatius was the founder of the Jesuit Order (Pope Francis is part of that order). Ignatius was wounded in war and while lying in bed for many months, he began to imagine himself interacting with Jesus and participating in the stories in the Bible. He imagined himself at the Crucifixion or at the dinner with

Mary and Martha or as the father welcoming the Prodigal Son home. These exercises were designed to put the participant into these stories as well. They changed my life. I gained insights and I learned the practice of reflection, which is part of what this book is all about.

I expect many people who are ill and who spend vast amounts of time lying in a hospital bed or can't have an active life could benefit from Active Imagination and could gain insight and wisdom and calm in the midst of difficult circumstances.

CHAPTER 14:

Clinging To God

*Faith is the virtue by which, clinging-to the
faithfulness of God, we lean upon him, so that
we may obtain what he gives to us.*
—William Ames, English philosopher

When we're healthy, it seems that our resources are strong enough to get us through. We feel on top of the world. We feel quite self-sufficient. We feel that we're doing just fine, thank you very much. But when we're ill, our resources are strained. We ask for *anything* that might be of help to us. We might cling to the wisdom of doctors. We might cling to the help of friends. We might cling to the hope of various types of diagnoses and prognoses and to every encouraging word said to us. We might cling to our own hope—that all is going to be all right again, perhaps very soon.

Healthy or sick, we often find that what we cling to doesn't pay off. Ultimately, there is only one place to cling to, and that is to God. We receive hope and resourcefulness and courage from some sense of that Presence. But how do we nurture the Presence of God and to lean into it? How do we continue to seek His friendly face?

Some get a sense of The Presence by being nourished through the words of the Bible. I'm not a literalist, but I do find a very Holy Spirit that glimmers through The Word of God. I have read the whole Bible at one time or another, and have spent years reading a Psalm almost daily. A favorite in time of trouble is Psalm 42: "My tears have been my food day and night."

Some get a sense of The Presence through prayer and meditation or by sitting still and feeling peaceful, taking deep breaths and quieting the mind, feeling the Light of God wash over them.

I'm a Quaker, and Quakers often talk about "waiting for The Light" or "sitting in The Light." Sometimes I think of basking in The Presence of God. Sometimes I'm able to let the Eternal Stillness have its way with me. I feel embraced by Mother God and Father God, that sense of the God who is everything and cannot be neatly put into categories or genders or some kind of human slots.

We cling to goodness. We cling to kindness. We cling to the love we receive from God and the comfort we receive from others. There is something encouraging about recognizing there is something to cling to. There are times when recognizing that we're vulnerable and needy is a good thing. When we're well, we can easily bypass our need. As babies, we cling, and it is perfectly all right. As people who are aware of our sickness and our brokenness, clinging to God is a very good thing to do.

CHAPTER 15:

Living In The In-Between

Life is not the way it's supposed to be, it's the way it is.
The way you cope with it is what makes the difference.
—Virginia Satir

When we think of our illness, we often think about what things were like before we got it and we imagine what things will be like after we get rid of it. We live in the "in between." It's easy for our minds to go to the past or the future, but is more difficult for us to live in the in-between place, in that process when things don't seem to be as good as they used to be and when they're not as good as we expect them to be later on.

It's not easy for us to recognize the value of the in-between. It doesn't seem that this in-between place is really what life is about so we do whatever we can so we don't have to deal with it.

We'd rather not dwell on this process. But if we can learn how to live in the in-between, for however long it takes us, we may be laying the foundation for a better life.

A few years ago, a friend of mine told me the story of a man who was imprisoned for seven years in a foreign country. He said for the first three years, he and his fellow prisoners talked about the past—about growing up in their families, about their hometowns, girlfriends, playing base-ball and football, their teachers, their homes, their schools. For the next three years they talked about their future—the parties they'd have when they were released, what it would be like to see their families again, the sports they'd play, and meals they'd eat, where they'd go on vacations. But in the seventh year, they stayed in the moment, notic-ing people and processes around them. They were released at the end of that year.

My friend believes the prisoners were released *as a re-sult* of living in the Present—Living in the In-Between. Another friend, who heard this story, said maybe they became more capable of bearing their burdens and could begin living in the Now. Another friend said, "Some kind people must have been praying and working for their re-lease." It wasn't necessarily cause and effect.

However, we look at it, these prisoners committed to the process just as we can do.

This is the Now, and this is how it is, and we can either choose to live in this Now or choose to toss our lives out for this period of time and not be here at all. We might choose not to live our lives fully even though we're fully here in this moment whether we like it or not. By not living in the Now, are we somehow wasting the moments of our lives? Are we, then, denying the meaning of our illness?

CHAPTER 16:

Some Theologies
Of Healing

We are not permitted to choose the frame of our destiny.
But what we put into it is ours.
—Dag Hammarskjold

During these years of struggling with my condition, I have talked to a number of my spiritual friends about their theology of healing. They have discussed their different ideas about how they figure out the meaning that gives them strength and how they heal, if they heal.

Several people I've talked to have medical conditions that are not going to get better. I had a client who is blind. He told me he considers this to be God's Will because so much good and opportunity to do good has come out of his accident. A friend of mine who has MS (multiple sclerosis) has used these same words, that this is God's will.

In both cases, there is a sense, not so much that God has punished them, but that God is using this for God's purpose.

Both are Christians. They're living evidence of the Bible verse: "In all things God works for the good of those who love Him." (Romans 8:28) Even our illnesses can be an opportunity to help others.

In many ways, great good came out of the tragedies and struggles that Christopher Reeve had to endure and Michael J. Fox continues to endure with Parkinson's disease. Joni Eareckson Tada has been an inspiration to millions, even though she is paralyzed and writes her books using a pencil in her mouth. These people are not just great witnesses *in spite of* their illnesses, but because of their illnesses.

A Will of God theology takes great faith and an ability to surrender ourselves totally to the movement of the Holy Spirit. I personally question this theology if it includes an image of God punishing us, or tripping us up, or making us fail as if God is somehow playing with our lives or manipulating us, even if it is for a higher purpose. The One who is Good doesn't do evil and the thought of a Bad God who kicks us around for His own purpose doesn't fit into my theological scheme of life! And I find no clear evidence of this God in experience or in Scripture. However, I find that many people with a God's Will theology have found a sense of peace and seem to have found the boundaries within this theology. In most cases, they don't believe God caused their suffering, but that God allowed it to continue for some greater purpose, knowing that His thoughts are not our thoughts and neither are His ways our ways (Isaiah 55:8.)

In Christianity, there is the belief in healing through prayer, laying on of hands, and even anointing. My friend Jana anointed me with oil from the Holy Land. I have rubbed the Holy dirt from Chimayo, New Mexico on my neck. I have done a thirty-day Novena because one of my Catholic friends told me I would get healed that way. I have been prayed over by a number of people from many different denominations. I believe in the possibility of miraculous healing— but it has not happened to me. The problem with this theology can be that it doesn't work for everyone. Those of us who are not healed in this way are often made to believe there is something wrong with our faith. We're at fault for not being healed. That's a heavy burden to bear.

Several other people I've met believe that our illness is a metaphor that is trying to teach us something. If we understand the lesson and the metaphor, we become healed. A friend of mine broke her arm and meditated about the meaning of her broken arm. She thought about what arms mean and what arms do—such as reaching out, embracing, pushing away or pulling toward, or used to elbow our way to what we want. My friend reflected for some time on the idea of reaching out and realized that she had been living within a very happy bubble, but had not been reaching and connecting enough with the broader public world. She once told me that she wanted to soar, but hadn't soared yet in her career. When her arm healed (which may or may not have healed faster than the arm would have healed without the metaphor) she began to reach out more and she began to soar in her professional and personal and spiritual life. Clearly, the metaphor was helpful to her, at the very least, in pointing the way to a new future. Jesus might have used the words here about becoming whole and becoming renewed and becoming a new creation, because that is what I saw happen to her.

I have reflected about the metaphor of *dystonia* and why my head turns to the left, as if it is turning away from something. My friend suggested that I think about words such as "turning," and "left," and "center" to find my metaphor, but I found nothing was clicking with those ideas. Recently, I have worked with the metaphor of "don't turn away," which has more resonance for me. I reflected on my life choices and realized my career has focused on the creative lives and spiritual lives of people, helping them reach for the highest in themselves in the world of imagination. My life has not been lived working with people who are ill or in pain or who are suffering. Compassion has been a more difficult quality for me to learn than creativity. But as my life has progressed, I wanted to become a more compassionate person and my medical problem, in a sense, has forced me to interact with many people who are hurting in one way or another. I have been telling myself, "Don't turn away from suffering, look it straight in the eye!" I also played with the metaphor of being more centered—a good metaphor for all of us. But neither metaphor healed me, at least not physically. Of course, some who believe in this theology might say I haven't yet found the right metaphor!

The danger, I believe, in this theology, can be that it is a "blame" theology, meaning that we got this medical problem because we were so flawed and imperfect that God caused it to happen for us to learn a lesson we weren't "getting" otherwise. The theology usually implies that as soon as we learn the lesson, we'll be healed. Of course, if this is true, we would all be zapped with some terrible disease because we're all imperfect and this metaphoric theology, if not understood with some sense of boundaries, can suddenly seem like the theology of Jonathan Edwards from the 1700s: *We are sinners in the hands of an angry God!* This is a God who is so determined to make us perfect that He is willing to zap us so we get the point. My response to that is, "Oh, dear! Mercy, mercy, mercy!"

I believe life intrinsically carries with it a wound or a brokenness that sets things awry. I believe in sin, but I also believe in blessings and grace and redemption that renews us and restores us. I don't believe this renewal happens without the work of the Holy Spirit, who I believe is always present. My wound is an expression that life is not perfect and that, when I believe that life is going to be absolutely perfect in every way, I'm being unrealistic. The brokenness in my body reminds me that we live as fallible and vulnerable human beings in need of being redeemed. For me, there is a juggling where I try to make sure I'm realistic about my brokenness and vulnerability and just as realistic about the Grace and Compassion and the Blessings and the Care that have been built into life by God the Creator and God the Restorer. Personally, I rather like the Garden of Eden story because it explains so many things about why we're out of harmony with God, with ourselves, with each other and with the earth. I'd like to go back there, whether it was a real place or not, because it echoes with that dream of being whole again.

My theology also has its dangers and its boundaries. It's possible to over-think it or to dwell on our wounds and not see Grace. It's also possible to affirm our Blessings and not recognize our Brokenness and need for God and to tell ourselves all is fine. Sin and Grace are usually paired together in the Scriptures, and I believe need to be paired together in our lives. Oh! It is so difficult to figure out—or at least to figure it out enough that our lives make sense to us.

CHAPTER 17:

Expanding Our Names For God

Many are the names of God and infinite the forms
through which He may be approached
—Ramakrisna (19th century Indian saint)

When I was first hurt, there was only one name of God that was of interest to me—Jehovah-Rapheka, the Lord Who Heals. I didn't care much about the Creator God, the Almighty God, or the Compassionate God, or the Alpha and the Omega, or the Holy One, or God our Father. I only cared about the aspect of God that was going to heal me. The Miracle Worker. The One who could make everything right. The One who fixed the things that went wrong. The One that would make me whole. Then, as months and years went on, it became clear that I was limiting God and that I was seeing God in such a small way that, even if

I were healed, I would not have been healed spiritually. I would still have had my blinders on. I would have still only seen God from my own personal, selfish perspective, and only see God in terms of one small function.

I've read many, many healing Scriptures that seemed to promise *immediate* healing for me. They are beautiful and encouraging words:

"But I will restore you to health and heal your wounds declares the Lord." (Jeremiah 30:17)

"Hope thou in God for I shall yet praise him, who is the health of my countenance, and my God." (Psalm 42:11 King James Version)

"That it might be fulfilled which was spoken saying, he Himself took our infirmities and bore our sickness." (Matthew 8:17)

"Therefore I say to you, whatever you desire, when you pray, believe that you receive them and you shall have them." (Mark 11:24)

"If you abide in you, you shall ask what you will, and it shall be done to you." (John 15:7, New King James Version)

"I have made you and I will carry you, I will sustain you and I will rescue you." (Isaiah 46:4)

"Then shall your light break forth your health shall spring forth speedily." (Isaiah 58:8, KJV)

It certainly sounds as if the Scriptures are promising me that what I ask for will be done to me, and that we will all live fairly happily ever after. But it doesn't seem to go that way, at least in terms of my timing. My timing is not God's timing, and things don't necessarily proceed as I want them to. I can't presume that "speedily" means "speedily" according to Webster's or my definition. Sometimes I've smiled and checked all my translations looking for loopholes.

On the other hand, Jacob wrestled with the Angel of the Lord and said, "I will not let you go unless you bless me." (Genesis 32:26) We remain in prayer and search God's Word and don't let God go, just as He doesn't let us go. God is the potter and we are the clay—and our illness is the wheel that goes round and round and doesn't stop just because we want it to.

I began to wonder what would happen if I stopped trying to put God into a box. What would happen if I stopped saying, "I only want you to be God the Healer and the Miracle Worker?"

I decided to make a list of how I *did* experience God, as opposed to what I did not experience. I wrote this list on Post-its on my mirror as I began to expand my names for God.

I thought about God as the One who suffers with us. I thought about Jesus as The Suffering Servant. Jesus didn't say a prayer and then everything was fine and he was speedily cured of his wounds and the bad things were speedily taken away from him. They weren't. He had to go through the crucifixion to get to the resurrection. I began to identify more with this idea that we do suffer and that we can be a suffering servant rather than acting like little children, kicking and screaming because things aren't going our way.

I realized I experienced God as The One Who Strengthens Me. My Rock. The One Who Sustains Me. My Helper and My Guide throughout the day. I began to feel that endurance was an underrated quality and I realized that I was enduring. God was The One Who Helped Me Endure. I realized there were many times when I would feel discouraged, but I would go to sleep and wake up and feel more possibilities with the new day. I felt strengthened to continue my therapies. I saw God as Hope. The One Who Overcomes Despair and Darkness, and makes it possible for me to move away from that sense of being overwhelmed.

There were, of course, many blessings in my life. But I was so focused on my problem that I was not always able to see the blessings that were given to me.

There are well over 300 names and descriptions of God in the Judeo-Christian religions. There are 99 names for God in Islam and many names for God in Hinduism. Many of these names are similar. These names and roles and functions of God will keep changing for us over the years. God is my Refuge in times of trouble. God is my Advocate. God is my Comforter in sorrow.

God is my Helper. My Shepherd. God is the Guide and Counselor who leads me to doctors and people who can help me. God is the great "I Am," the One who permeates all things.

If we believe that God's hands are directing our lives and that God is The Giver of All Good Things, then obviously everything good that comes to us—from finding good doctors to having friends who support us to having a good spiritual community to seeing the flowers bloom and the birds sing—comes from the hand of God. The hand of God has more than five fingers.

I began to also realize that the most important thing in this journey is not my healing, but it is whether I love God. I realized I really didn't love God enough. I felt I tried to do the will of God and I tried to be obedient to God and I tried to talk to God and to wait upon God, but I wondered if I really *loved* God. As I prayed, I felt as if God was reminding me of the Bible verse that says, "We love because He first loved us," (I John 4:19) I began to recognize that I was trying to see God as The Beloved, but I also had to recognize that God was the Lover. Whether we get healed or not is really beside the point. There was only one thing required of us—to love The Lord Your God with all your heart, with all your soul, and with all your strength, and to love your neighbor as yourself." (Luke 10:27) That is the challenge whether we are hurt, healing, or whole.

What a difficult thing to do when we're suffering, because suffering takes up our whole mind-set and fills all available pores. Making room for God, learning to see the Hand of God, and loving God, can be as great a challenge as the actual physical or mental struggle. Yet, the physical and mental problems can often be lessened through our spiritual commitment if we don't give up on God and ourselves.

PART THREE:

Surrender, But Don't Give Up

CHAPTER 18:

Surrender Versus Resignation

In one sense, the road back to God is a road of moral effort, of trying harder and harder. But in another sense it is not trying that is ever going to bring us home. All this trying leads up to the vital moment at which you turn to God and say, "You must do this. I can't."
—C.S. Lewis, Mere Christianity

What is demanded of us? There are verses in the Bible, and in much spiritual literature, that talk about the need to surrender. If we spend all of our time fighting and resisting and being pushed into our therapies so that all our mind can think about is getting better, we become frenetic and the peace that we need in order to heal is no longer with us. Yet, it seems that if we surrender to our illness, we're giving up.

At one point in my illness, I told one of my friends that I was trying to learn to surrender and she was horrified. She said that I must not surrender to illness and must not think that this is all right. In a sense, illness is the enemy and we need to keep fighting it. Yet I felt some kind of relief when I considered surrendering, and this relief was reversed after talking to this friend. After much thinking, I realized there was a difference between surrender and resignation. I had not become resigned to my illness or resigned to the fact that I would never improve or get better, but I was trying to achieve a sense of letting go, a sense of release, a sense of recognizing this is how things were and this is how the flow of the river was going right now, and there was a point that I had to learn to go with the flow.

My spiritual director suggested to me that I might actually say to the illness, "Welcome, what do you have to teach me? What can I learn from this situation?" My friend Devo said, "God, I'm in a healing challenge. Please guide me to the lessons I can learn from it. I welcome the light and release the dark."

Surrender might mean coming to terms with our situation. Surrender might mean recognizing that this is how things are at this point. Surrender might recognize that this is the New Normal. Surrender might mean getting into the rhythm of our illness. It might mean we recognize that there are certain processes going on and we can no longer live our daily lives in the same order with the same structure and with the same determination we used to have to achieve other life goals. There is something else going on and attention must be paid to this fact. We try to

get into the new rhythm, recognizing that even the rhythm
of illness might have something to teach us about slowing
down, watching the flowers grow, nurturing ourselves, letting go of some areas in life that create irritations, trying
to take more moments for our spouse, friends, and pets,
and letting a few other things slide. And always listening
for the Still Small Voice and trying to see the Hand of God.

CHAPTER 19:

What Must I Do To Help God Heal Me?

The reason why many are still troubled, still seeking, still making little forward progress, is because they haven't yet come to the end of themselves. We're still trying to give orders, and interfering with God's work within us.
—A.W. Tozer

It was not happening quickly and full recovery certainly had not yet happened. I started a morning prayer, asking God "what must I do today to help you heal me?" The prayer depended on my wanting to be healed and being willing to do what I had to do for my healing, but also recognizing that if God wanted me to be healed, I had to team up with God and be willing to do my part. I realized there were some mornings I didn't want to ask that question because I didn't feel like being committed to my part of my healing. I was too tired, I didn't feel like doing my therapies that day, and besides, I was in a grumpy mood. I had very little faith that they were going to work that day and thought maybe it didn't matter whether I did them or not. (I always did them but I sometimes did them begrudgingly!) But I had to learn that God's work is cumulative. A seed doesn't grow in a day.

I really wanted to eat what I wanted to eat even though it was on my list of things not to eat. Since I had two different medical problems, I had learned that certain foods were not good for cancer and certain foods were beneficial. I wanted sugar, but my healing was dependent on not having sugary sweets. There were some days when I really wanted the whole Lindt dark chocolate bar with raspberry filling, but on those days, I was not helping God do God's work.

On mornings when I had the courage to ask God to help me be committed, I would usually feel guided. Sometimes that guidance helped me remember a therapy I hadn't done or gave me the willpower to not eat the bar of dark chocolate, or gave me the energy for a walk. I tried to be more attentive to these leadings. I tried to tune in so when I got a leading, rather than saying I would do it later, I would try to respond immediately. I began to discover that there were leadings on many different levels.

I began to ask the question in a broader way. It wasn't just about, "What must I do today to help You heal me from dystonia or cancer?" Instead, it was, "What must I do today to help You heal me, God?" With this question, I began to recognize that healing was much broader than my neck not turning or the cancer cells disappearing. I wondered what I should do today to not be stressed and frustrated which can feed both cancer and dystonia. I wondered what I should do today to be less irritated or to be less bothered or less impatient. I wondered what I should do today to help me heal spiritually.

On the other hand, I didn't want to live my life by rules. I didn't want to feel as if someone was giving me orders. With my illness, I had less freedom than I had before and yet, suddenly my life was more stressed because I had to keep remembering to do my therapies morning, noon, and night and I had to keep remembering what I had to eat or not eat. Just when I needed to reduce stress to heal, I felt I had more stress and more frustration. I felt like my life was a bunch of marching orders and rules. It was so easy to see God and my doctors as autocrats, telling me what to do. I tried very hard to be obedient, but I didn't feel spontaneous or free. I was not moving with the flow of life, which seemed more important than following the rules of life.

I began to start my day with a willingness to let the Holy Spirit work inside of me. I called on the Holy Spirit to move me in a spontaneous way, as opposed to thinking of God as my "general." I believed this would help me be more willing to do my therapies and my healthy diet. Sometimes when I ate, I would try to think about how I would feel later if I had that dessert. Perhaps I might not feel good or not sleep as well, and that motivated me. (And fewer calories couldn't hurt!)

When I called on Wisdom, I found her to be light and

kind and embracing. She filled me in a way that seemed to take the mean and snarky parts of me away so I could see the bigger picture. I felt enriched as she began to attune me to the different layers of healing.

I'm not totally convinced that change is so much a decision on our part as a "leading" that we say "yes" to. If the Spirit is leading us into certain actions, the actions will be freeing and enjoyable. When I tried to take a morning walk because I felt like I was supposed to, it didn't work. When I felt led to take the morning walk, I began to enjoy it and it fit quite well into my schedule. I live in the beautiful Colorado mountains and what is not to love about the birds singing and the thousands of trees glistening in the morning sun?

I also have discovered that change is natural. It is not unusual for someone who has had cancer to *want* to change. I have talked to a number of people who had cancer who told me when they finished their treatment, they felt the necessity to change something immediately. My friend Devo painted her living room with more subdued colors to create calm versus excitement. She said afterwards she missed her bedazzling colors and added them back in. Rose told me after she finished her cancer treatment she had to buy a convertible. She said her friend had to buy a pick-up truck. Both of these can be symbols of strength and adventure. My mother had to go to Europe. I found that I *needed* to replace my casual everyday dishware. We previously had Western dishes with bucking broncos on them and I realized they no longer had much meaning for me.

This kind of change is not a wish, it's a need. I learned it was important to listen to that driving force, although I'm very pleased that my dishware is far less expensive than the Corvette! (I'm developing a desire to take a cruise, but I think it's still just a *want* rather than a *need!*)

One would hope that the changes that come on many levels are also bringing back that which is good in our lives that might have been left behind at some point. Sometimes that goodness has to do with friendships that are renewed, or having more appreciation for the music we loved as a child, or seeing life with innocent eyes once again. Sometimes we choose something new to fulfill us because we've learned something about fulfillment. We may go to a new church that nurtures us more than the church we were going to. We may gain new friends who have qualities we never noticed before the illness. We can try not to delay these good things, but instead, say "yes" to change.

CHAPTER 20:

In The Midst Of Being Healed

Although the world is full of suffering, it is also full of the overcoming of it.
—Helen Keller

We hope and sometimes expect that our healing will be quick. When we read about the healings of Jesus, people were healed with a touch, with a word, with an action, and the healing all seemed to take place within seconds. As we pray for healing, we keep hoping for that miracle.

I wondered if healing might be going on in my life and if I simply wasn't aware of it. In many cases, people who go through rehabilitation can see a result within a few days. In the case of dystonia, or any kind of brain-related physical or mental or neurological problem, the movement forward is so imperceptible that there seems to be little cause and effect.

If someone asks me if I'm getting better, I can tell them whether I'm getting worse, but I usually am not able to perceive if I'm getting better or how much better I'm getting. There are occasional markers, but often I have to trust the doctors who do various tests and tell me that the brain is stabilizing. I can identify particular activities that I'm now able to do; things that I couldn't do six months ago. I'm more able to reach out to others. I'm more interested in leaving the house and doing some fun things. When I go to a movie theater I don't have to sit as far left in the audience as I used to. I can take longer walks. But all of these good changes are compared with three or six months or a year ago, not day to day.

And yet, I'm being healed. I have presumed that the work of God would be something a little more miraculous than it is and much faster. I'm now recognizing that there are people in my life—doctors and friends and therapists and my spiritual director—who are helping me through my healing, and that I can't doubt that God is healing me.

Sometimes we recognize the work of healing because other people recognize it, even when we don't. I have a dear friend with a brain injury. Brenda W. wasn't able to walk out of the doctor's office alone when I first met her. She was too dizzy. One day, she said goodbye to the doctor at the doctor's door and started walking out the building. I called to her and I said, "You're walking on your own. I can't believe the progress—this is marvelous!" Soon, we were able to have lunches out which she hadn't done in years. Then we had trial runs to see if she could drive from her house to my house with me standing by in case I had to go pick her up. Like me, she needed to be reminded healing was happening.

Some time ago, I was introduced to another *dystonia* patient who looked at me and said, "I can't believe how good you look. I hope I can look that good in a few years." And the doctor then mentioned to the other patient that I was not always like this.

When not clearly going backwards, God is undoubtedly moving us forward. It is up to us to work with the Spirit and not against it. For me, that means to be more in touch with my body even when the cues are subtle. There are clearly times I know something is not working, and I've been able to e-mail my doctors to tell them an exercise seems to be pushing me backwards right now. They have quickly been able to tell me to stop it or to tweak it or to cut it from my routine.

Improvement is slow and often takes months or years. I'm learning to pray that I will be in touch with God and that I also will be moved and guided by God. I pray to have the endurance to continue doing my therapies and to feel God's encouragement so I don't get discouraged and despair. I pray to stay in tune with God's power so I can stay as quiet and calm and centered as possible so that I don't work against the work of The Healer. This is a partnership and I pray that I will carry my part. I have more than once accused God of not carrying His part, but my self-righteousness is quickly broken down when I see ways I don't cooperate with the Movement of God for my life. I have gradually realized that the Holy Spirit is working every day to bring me to wholeness and I have a big role in helping attain this goal.

CHAPTER 21:

Get Well Quick

Me and You is friends,
You smile, I smile.
You hurt, I hurt.
You cry, I cry.
You jump off bridge, I going to miss you!
—from a greeting card on Google

Have you ever noticed how uncomfortable friends seem to be with our illness? They're frustrated because we're not yet healed, and they wonder what advice or magic bullet or tidbit of wisdom they can give us that will take away their frustration over our frustration. They wonder what we are, or are not, doing to get better. They wonder if we have researched the best doctors and are settling for second best. Might we be putting up resistances to our healing? Maybe we really, really don't want to be healed and are clinging to our illness for some benefit that we clearly must get over.

A friend once blamed me for the length of time it was taking me to get healed. I told her that if she had an idea about how to get better by tomorrow morning, I'd be happy to do it. She didn't and admitted that she was not an expert on neurology or the brain, but she did think I should be allowing the Spirit to come through more. Yes, of course.

I have wondered about this reaction to another's illness. I think people are afraid to be around suffering. The lack of resolution is very hard on others—and ourselves. If we can't solve our problems, then maybe if they had the same problem, they wouldn't be able to solve it either. That is terrifying. It is the ultimate out-of-control feeling and we must feel that we have control in this Universe.

We're sometimes told by people who are supposedly spiritual that we're in control of what our brain thinks and if we only get the brain thinking more positively and take control of our illness, we'll be "all better." They tell us we aren't taking responsibility for our illness and we aren't thinking enough positive thoughts. My friend thinks positive thoughts and she doesn't have this disease. Therefore, if I thought more positive thoughts, I also wouldn't have this disease. At the same time, she still has her physical problems that haven't gone away in spite of her positive thinking, prayers, and meditations. I can relate.

The sense of frustration with our illness is so difficult that friends have different ways of dealing with it. Some people separate because they don't want to be around us. Others confront us—we need to get on the ball and fix it!

Others give advice—have you tried this or that? Others ask questions such as, "How are you doing?" Sometimes they walk away before you finish the answer. When I suggested to my friend that she ask me that question rather than blame me, she answered, "I don't want to know because you'll give me a 25 minute answer." I said to her, "Of course. It's complicated." I then suggested we have a short-hand for questions and she could ask, "Could you give me the short hand answer of how you're doing?" "Yes," I answer. "I'm doing better today than 6 months ago." "Oh, good." What a relief to her! "Well, I'm off to the gym," she says.

And so it goes. Our suffering is our own—and we keep turning it over to God. Keep trying to be a compliant patient. Keep praying. Keep bonding with friends who understand. Keep questioning and doing the best we know how to do. Keep hoping and working toward a complete healing— which may, or may not, happen.

CHAPTER 22:

Learning The Virtues

*Hope, like every virtue, is a choice that
becomes a habit, that becomes spiritual muscle memory.
It's a renewable resource for moving through
life as it is, not as we wish it to be.*
—Krista Tippett, from *Becoming Wise: An Inquiry into
the Mystery and Art of Living*

When we're well, Virtues may not seem essential. We're doing just fine. Does anything really change because we're virtuous?

The book of *Galatians* in the New Testament lists the fruits of the spirit: joy, peace, patience, kindness, goodness, truthfulness, gentleness, self-control, and love (Galatians 5). The early Christian Church not only talked about the Seven Deadly Sins of envy, pride, gluttony, lust, anger, sloth and greed, but also talked about the seven virtues—kindness, humility, temperance, chastity, patience, diligence, and charity. The Greek philosophers listed the virtues of prudence, justice, restraint, and courage. St. Paul, in the letter of *I Corinthians*, recorded the virtues of faith, hope, and love.

In our normal lives, when we're relatively healthy, we can often get by without being very virtuous. We go along with life, we get along fairly well with other people, and there is a certain flow to our lives that doesn't demand of us excessive amounts of those qualities that can bring out the best in us. But when we're ill, we are tested. One of my doctors once said to me, "This will take every ounce of patience you have," and it's been true. My reservoirs of patience have, more than once, been totally exhausted, only to somehow find another resource that keeps me going.

I really think that the bravest people on earth are those who are ill and manage to get by daily. Every morning they're able to see something good in life, with a smile on their face, and still interact in a positive way with other people.

When my sister was ill with ALS and we were quite sure that she would die within two or three years, she shone with grace and beauty. She encountered her daily trials with patience and fortitude and sweetness, which was a wonder to behold. Even when she died at the age of 62, and people expressed their sadness about this tragic event, I thought of what a witness she had been. When people talk about "dying well" as well as "living well," we realize that there is a certain quality that goes into facing these tremendous physical and mental struggles and difficulties and challenges.

We're asked to pull out these qualities, not just because they're good qualities to have, but because when we're ill, it's almost impossible to get by daily without them. Every morning we wake up and we have to bring these qualities to the forefront. We're challenged to make this a daily occurrence.

There is another quality that is demanded of us: in order to live well, there has to be some exchange of goodness, love, and kindness from us to another person. Our learned virtues need to be shared. The problem here is that we're so busy caring for ourselves, dealing with the everyday and every-minute necessities, that it's difficult to give.

The need for being kind and loving and caring for others in the midst of our trials doesn't mean we have to carry another or even be excessively attentive to them to the detriment of what is needed for ourselves. But we cannot keep going through this illness without some exchange of care and concern and kindness for others.

When my sister became ill, her husband suggested she give smiles and kindness back to her caregivers. I had not thought of that, but then realized care-givers give every day, put their skills, heart, and souls into helping, and many times get a hurt, frustrated, serious, and even grumpy patient.

I wondered if I could become a good and kind patient, giving to others as I was given to by others. I remembered this idea when I went through twenty sessions of radiation for Stage 2A breast cancer in early 2016. For the first few days, I was too freaked out by the big, spooky, looming machine to be nice. Dystonia affects the part of my brain related to claustrophobia so any enclosure can cause me anxiety. It's another special side "gift" of this problem. After a few days, with a little help from Xanax for the first few days, I tried to do an attitude adjustment and asked myself what I could give. I learned the names of receptionists and therapists. I tried to smile more, up my sense of humor, notice other patients, say little prayers for them at times, rejoice with them, and clap my hands when they were finishing their twenty or thirty sessions. If I saw a patient waiting in the small waiting area, I sat two seats away, said, "Hello," and if the person engaged, tried to be a good listener or talked to them. I couldn't do this when deeply into my own anxiety, but as I got a wee bit better, it became easier.

I then e-mailed about 20 friends who had asked if they could help and let them know how they could help: I asked them to send e-mails instead of calling, bring food if they wished, or to take me to radiation appointments to give Peter a break. I kept them informed of my progress, since, in my case, writing comes naturally to me and it was my preferred method of communication.

I gave what I could and tried not to put a trip on myself. When it was over, I contributed to the Memorial Hospital's Cancer Fund in honor of my six radiation therapists who received certificates of thanks.

I kept trying to remember: "Care for your care-givers," but also tried to live under the Grace of Forgiveness. This was an opportunity to practice grace, patience, forgiveness of self and others, and self-control, if possible.

I sometimes got snarky, lost my sense of humor, and

put on a serious face that couldn't have been fun to be around.

Through the trial of illness, I have created a list of my own personal favorite virtues: courage, valor, fortitude, endurance, patience, hope, faith, perseverance, compassion for others, an ability to recognize and receive blessings, and an ability to receive love and goodness in all its forms.

I'm amazed, as I observe how our resources continue to be renewed. I'm uplifted as I observe courage and remarkable endurance.

We keep on going because there is this Spirit that we can draw on that teaches us the virtues, and that upholds us.

CHAPTER 23:

Reflecting Light In Our Brokenness

"Wait for the Light," "Wait in the Light,"
—from Quaker Faith and Practice

When we're broken and wounded, we might think of the image that we see through a glass darkly. We don't often see things clearly because we're in pain and our eyes are clouded over and we're so looking inward that we're not able to look outward. Things are not bright and sunny and clear and clean. Sometimes we feel we don't know what side is up. Sometimes we feel as if we walk around in a cloud. Sometimes we feel as if we cannot see anything clearly enough to make a rational decision or if there's not enough light out there; and everything is dark and sometimes even formless. We cannot make out the path or make out the direction in which we might go. Is the right or the left better?

We learn to look for those moments of light and clarity; to appreciate them and recognize them and often give a prayer of gratitude for them. It is difficult to stop the light, even when we're in a dark place. The light eventually comes through.

Sometimes we have to look for the slivers of light to guide us because we don't have enough to see the whole vista or the whole panorama. We've probably all seen how light comes through a stained-glass window and forms patterns on a carpet or on a wall. Even a small window of light can cast a large pattern.

I was in Sweden one summer. Scandinavian countries are very dark during the winter. There are certain places above the Arctic Circle where the sun never rises—it stays on the horizon all day long. Yet, in the summer, the sun shines for 20 or more hours a day. Since I wanted to make sure I got a good night's sleep, and didn't wake at the crack of dawn (4:00 a.m.) I would close my curtains very carefully so slivers of light did not come through to wake me. I would put a chair against the curtain to hold the curtain as close to the wall as possible. Then I would put another chair on the other side of the curtain to make sure that light didn't come through. I would put a table against the middle of the curtains so that the room stayed dark. But I noticed I couldn't keep the light out. No matter what I did hoping to sleep late, it was not going to work. The light will come through.

Just as we can't stop the light we also don't stop being slivers of light to others, in spite of our brokenness.

Many, many people who are ill or hurt have often heard other people say to them, "You are such an inspiration to me. I can't believe how you were able to go through this!" Or, "You are such a witness. You actually helped me get through my therapies last week because I realize how hard you work at your therapies." We think that we can be glimmers of light only when we're better. But actually, we can become reflections of light in our brokenness in the same way that a broken window pane or a smudged window pane doesn't stop the light.

So too, the Light can't be stopped from getting through to us. There are innumerable stories of people in concentration camps who would stop in awe at the song of birds or the pink and golden rays of a sunset. Often, people in a hospital in the midst of great pain, gratefully acknowledge the comfort and kindness of a nurse or a visitor who brings the Light into the room.

It becomes so important to us that we look for the Light in the midst of our illness. We can recognize there is Light within ourselves that is helpful to other people, just as the Light from other people is helpful to us. In the midst of the worst suffering, there are always slivers of light.

CHAPTER 24:

Becoming Whole

Fear not: believe only, and she shall be made whole.
—Luke 8:50 (KJV)

Anyone who doesn't believe in sin and woundedness and brokenness has either not been reading the morning papers or has never had an illness. There may be a few people on this planet who have had a happy and smooth life every day and have never had any of the troubles that most people encounter. Perhaps these are the people who die before problems get to them! But I expect the totally happy life is very, very rare. Our new theology might make us more aware of the fact that woundedness is interwoven into the human condition. That's what the story of Adam and Eve is all about. You don't have to take it literally to believe that something has happened within human life and that somewhere within the human condition there is a brokenness that human life carries with it.

In the book of *Genesis*, we're told that this brokenness

affects us in many ways. For the woman, she now has pain in childbirth. For the man, when he tills the soil it will no longer give him plants without sweat and toil. No longer will things go so smoothly and so beautifully and so harmoniously as they did in the Garden of Eden. Our relationship with our Creator, which was peaceful, has also changed. The sense of a harmonious relationship with God got flawed and broken with The Fall.

Yet, there is also entrenched in life the possibility of renewal and redemption and becoming whole, because we would like to have faith and hope about the future. My friend Brenda L., who also has dystonia, told me that when she was a child, she went to a summer camp for disabled kids. It was Camp HeHoHa, short for Health, Hope, and Happiness.

Like Happy Camper Brenda, we hope for that possibility of harmony and balance and wholeness and yet, in many cases, we don't feel it or find it or live it. We live in brokenness and our bodies and our minds feel it. Yet, we still search for meaning, and the meaning doesn't let us go.

Perhaps we have hope that one day we'll be healed or hope that in spite of our condition, our lives will still be filled with love, joy, peace, and the strength and patience to bear our situation.

In Christian theology, and in most of the healing stories, Jesus healed a person and it is said, "He made him whole." The idea of healing is never just a matter of a physical or mental healing— there is something else that happens as a result of the healing that is even more important.

As I live with my physical problem, I sometimes wonder about the order of this kind of healing. In most cases, wholeness comes *as a result* of the healing. However at times, Jesus forgave the person first (thereby making the person whole) and *then* healed the affliction. Sometimes I have wondered whether the order is usually reversed so that spiritual healing and wholeness comes *before* we're physically and mentally healed, as if part of the healing process asks us to pay attention to wholeness, which is the real goal of healing. I wonder if our work is to try to become whole *in spite of* the physical or mental problem we carry with us.

How does this seem to work? If we have a physical injury, we're probably doing therapies and exercises in order to heal the injury. While we're doing them, we're also strengthening ourselves as whole people. Some of us, who may not have exercised a great deal before, suddenly find that we have to exercise in order to cure our injury. In that process, we learn to be people who exercise. We learn to take care of our physical bodies as well as to be people who become stronger so that when we're healed, we have the strength to hold the healing. We have actually become whole people first.

In my case, I was far more in tune with the intricacies of my mind than the subtleties of my body. I have had to learn to be in tune with my body to know daily how therapies are affecting me so I can give feedback to the doctors. I have begun to see how subtle life decisions affect my body. I have to be willing to change in order to be healed and willing to commit daily to this change. I become easily stressed which makes my brain spin and obsess and not let go of negative unresolved thoughts. I then chew on the problem, looking at it in many creative ways, like a pit bull that won't let go. At those moments, I need Inner Peace mighty fast, but it won't come because I can't calm myself immediately. It's the condition. For me, becoming whole means a sense of quiet and peace.

As I write this, I'm in my hotel room in Houston waiting to go to the Clinic for the day. I'm listening to nature tapes, occasionally holding my tiny, three-inch square traveling prayer "shawl" given to me by the United Church of Christ in Colorado Springs, reflecting on the Bible verse at the beginning of this chapter. My breathing has slowed. My neck is only a bit off-center. In this moment, I have some sense of feeling whole. Perhaps other moments of healing will come as well.

If we have a mental illness, we might find that working with the therapist actually makes us stronger and more willing to confront a problem or to have greater insight. We might become whole *and then* have the mental illness healed in that process. When we're mentally healed, we become stronger people because we have learned fortitude and wisdom and insight during the process.

Yet, how difficult this is. Here we are, struggling to get by daily, perhaps exercising to rehabilitate, taking a pill to reduce pain, remembering to do a therapy, to go to appointments, to file for insurance, to research another medical modality—and with all of this—we have to also deal with our spiritual lives. Dealing with our disabilities already seems like too much. Now we also have to fix our relationship with God! But I'm wondering if this is really the easy part.

I have noticed in myself very subtle attitudes that resist healing and resist the Holy Spirit. I get angry at God for not healing me faster and then don't take time to express my anger so God can be in dialogue with me and comfort me. I don't take the time to do a therapy and wonder if it's really important—thereby not allowing it to do its work. I decide to eat something that has negative effects on me, because at that moment, I care more about the taste than I do about my healing. Sometimes my desire for something else is greater than my desire to be made whole.

I'm trying, in those moments, to say, "So sorry—help me!" It is difficult to be whole—it can be even more difficult to *want* to be whole. Perhaps, we come to the conclusion that any healing is not complete if only the ailment is healed; we need our spirit and faith to be healed as well.

CHAPTER 25:

Work For Good

Turn your wounds into wisdom.
—Oprah Winfrey

Many of my Christian friends, who have stood by me through this ordeal, have often quoted the verse from Romans 8: "And we know that in all things God works for the good of those who love Him, who have been called according to His purpose." For some time, I had come to the conclusion that there were many good things in life in spite of the problems I was encountering. But I didn't see how the negative things could work for good.

Recently, I have begun to understand how things can all work for the Good. I have begun to see that everything in life is capable of being redeemed and that when God sheds light on even the bad things, they begin to change. Some of that can come as a result of what we learn from our illness. For us to grow in some way as a result of this illness is a positive thing and it may be that without it, we wouldn't have grown. We do tend to be stubborn people sometimes and we need to be pushed and shoved to greater development in spite of our resistance and even though we yell out, "No, I don't want to go there. Don't make me!" I understand that even challenging places can be healing. I have begun to see that the Dark Places can illuminate the human condition and help us understand more realistically and see more clearly and more courageously what life is about. I think these Dark Places can actually take the blinders off and can be redeemed because we have a more profound and deeper view of life. We learn not to be so afraid of the Suffering Dark when we see others who are hurting or wounded. Instead of running away from them, we move with compassion toward them. Our illnesses lead to us to do something good for others and to be more capable of moving into the depths of life without fear.

CHAPTER 26:

Waiting For Forty Years

My ancestors wandered lost in the wilderness
for forty years because even in biblical times,
men would not stop to ask for directions
—Elayne Boosler

In the Exodus story, when the Israelites left Egypt, they crossed the Red Sea and they went into the Wilderness, waiting to go to the Promised Land. They expected to go immediately and yet they were in the Wilderness for forty years. Only a very few made it. You may ask, "Why did it take forty years?" It took time for the Israelites to go through the changes necessary to *become* the Chosen People, to become the people who were capable of going to the Promised Land and who had acquired the mind-set which made them able to accept the blessing of the Promised Land.

When I graduated from seminary, the president of my seminary said, "You know you're on the way to the

Promised Land by the fear that you feel when you take the first step." We are all trying to get to the Promised Land. For those of us who are ill, the Promised Land is the land of health and wholeness. But we might ask, "How do we become a person capable of walking into the Promised Land and doing whatever Chosen People are called to do?"

We often don't know how long it will take. We don't know at what point we'll step into the Promised Land and become new people. We don't know if we'll make it. Maybe we'll get to the border, get a glimpse of what could be, and don't get to go. Maybe, like some of the Israelites, we won't make it in this lifetime. But we're called to keep moving forward. And if we feel fear, we know it can be part of taking the first step.

PART FOUR:

Hope In Spite Of

CHAPTER 27:

Changing Habits

I define hope as distinct from optimism or idealism.
It has nothing to do with wishing. It references
reality at every turn and reveres the Truth.
It lives open-eyed and wholeheartedly with the
darkness that is woven ineluctably into the
Light of Life and sometimes seems to overcome it.
—Krista Tippett, from the book *Becoming Wise: An*
Inquiry into the Mystery and Art of Living

It's very difficult to change habits and it's very difficult to know if there are any habits to be changed. It's often said with cancer that people need to make a lifestyle change to get well. This is undoubtedly true for many other illnesses because we consciously or unconsciously keep exacerbating them with things we do. These may have been part of our life before the illness that may have partially caused the illness and may continue to threaten us. Yet, often these habits have been embedded in the pattern of our lives.

I have always been an achiever. I worked hard at school and worked hard at starting a business— perhaps too hard. The doctors have some thoughts that all those years of trying to get a business started, working against the storm that kept trying to blow me backwards and off course, caused stress in my body. Perhaps, when I had the small traffic accident, it triggered the dystonia as if it were a latent problem ready to be pushed into expression.

I was predisposed to cancer because my mother, an aunt, and a cousin had cancer. It is possible that the stress that caused dystonia may have also had some influence on the cancer.

I began meditating on what dystonia and cancer have in common. Both of them are problems that are about being "stuck." Cancer cells get stuck in a tumor and with dystonia, my head gets stuck in a certain position.

When I asked myself what got stuck in my life, at first I couldn't find an answer because most people who know me would say, "You are probably one of the least stuck people I have ever met." I don't procrastinate. I make things happen. I'm a do-er. Then I thought, "Am I holding on too tightly to an idea or a relationship?" Ah! I can see that I hold on to business relationships too long, because I believe that all problems are solvable and that things will be just fine if we can talk about them. How very silly of me! I also tend to see the best in people and I can see that when things work well they work very well. But when they don't work well, they drive me nuts. That's not good for either cancer or dystonia.

I wondered if I were trying to control people. Then, it occurred to me that I sometimes allow other people to control me. On the whole, I'm a very self-directed person. I get ideas and I follow them through. Other people sometimes get ideas about what I should be doing and I sometimes listen to them, even when I know they're not right for me. Then I also realized that I work faster and am more organized than most people are. That has always been the case. My mother was once asked, "What is the difference between your two daughters?" My mother lovingly answered, "Holly is so slow you can't stand it, and Linda is so fast you can't stand it!" She called it right.

I have found that when I get entangled in something, it's very difficult to get untangled. Usually, the entanglements are so complicated that it's much like untangling 100 yards of string where even the string doesn't know where the beginning and the end are. This usually means I have not respected my path, which usually moves quickly down the trail without a whole lot of obstacles. I usually have a clear goal in mind and I have some sense of how to get there. If I don't have to whack through trees or I don't have to wade through the swamps and the molasses, I can go at a fairly peaceful pace. So when I have somebody holding me back or getting in the way, I sometimes don't respect myself enough to affirm my own way of doing things.

I then began thinking about freedom. Freedom is not going on a safari if you're afraid of lions. Freedom is not deciding to parachute from a plane if you're afraid of heights. Freedom is about doing those things that loosen you up and give you joy. Freedom should also bring a sense of peace.

Freedom can mean standing in a place where we can say, "This is my place to stand and I have the right to stand here." I love it when people say, "Go girl!" or they say, "Good work, keep it up," which affirms my path and helps me to not only get healed but to stay with the patterns that will keep me healed.

CHAPTER 28:

The New Normal

*(Jesus said) Therefore do not be anxious about
tomorrow, for tomorrow will be anxious for itself.
Sufficient for the day is its own trouble.*
—Matthew 6:34

Being in a state of illness is part of the New Normal.
There is a period of time when we have to stay with the
process and recognize that this is how it is for this part of
our lives. Instead of negating it, we stand in that moment
of living. We recognize it.

A big part of my New Normal is the hours of therapies
I do every day. Every morning when I become conscious,
I begin doing therapies for my brain. I spend 30 minutes
in bed with oxygen while listening to Pachabel's *Canon in
D* and meeting Jesus in the garden. I sometimes counted
backwards by increments of 13, 14, 15, 16, and 17, usually
starting with 300, or so, which is a real brain tester, but it
would quiet the spasms in my neck. I do various exercises

when I get up—marching in place, waving my arms back and forth over my head like the snow angels we used to do as children. I then go downstairs and walk up and down the driveway reciting the letters of the alphabet, thinking one letter and saying the next letter aloud and hoping the neighbors don't notice my strange behavior!

I come back into the house and do some eye and neck exercises. I look at photographs of cute dogs and cats, which makes my neurons smile. For two years, I did Sodoku every morning to activate the weaker (and more mathematical) part of my brain. For a short period of time, I wore a coat hanger on my head (!) for about two minutes at a time. It put pressure on a certain part of my skull. At one point, I was going on a 10-hour plane ride and my doctor suggested that I wear it periodically that day. She added, "You'll never see these people again, so what does it matter if you're wearing a coat hanger on your head?" She didn't realize the number of times I have met people on airplanes that I know! Wouldn't it be embarrassing if word got out that Linda, the author and script consultant, was truly, truly weird? Needless to say, I disobeyed the doctor!

Throughout the day, I repeat various exercises. When at the computer (which I now seldom use since the computer light is difficult for the neurons we're trying to calm) I wear rose-colored glasses—not a bad idea!—which is the color that slows the neurons. Sometimes I spin in a swivel chair or follow a laser with my eyes. Before I go to sleep, I breathe oxygen for twenty minutes, while listening to Nature Sounds, which relaxes me and I'm told does good things to the brain. Each exercise may only take seconds or a minute or two, but every repetition is important. And all this while not stressing over my therapies! And thankfully, these therapies, even the ones that sound silly, have helped me improve.

These exercises change somewhat as my brain heals and as I gain more strength, but doing the therapies is my New Normal. Then I have to do my cancer therapies, which are designed to give mobility to the left arm from the operation: pretending to take a sword from my right hip and drawing it toward my left. Lying on a big ball and pretending I'm flying while flapping my arms in various directions. Pretending to take a worm out of my right ear and dropping it on the floor to my left (I'd rather take a rabbit out of my hat!) Yet all these exercises for dystonia and cancer healing have been helpful.

I have found the New Normal has some benefits. I'm forced to go slower in my life. I have learned to putter. I exercise more. I try to forgive myself for forgetting something (sometimes my brain has a black hole. Things disappear.) I try to forgive myself for not being as responsive to friends as I want to. Peter and I have a sweet time to talk while I do my oxygen at night. Perhaps there is just as much goodness now, as ever before.

CHAPTER 29:

In Spite Of

We must be willing to let go of the life we planned so as to have the life that is waiting for us.
—Joseph Campbell

In spite of the darkness there is light. In spite of what seems like a curse, there are still blessings. In spite of being overwhelmed, there is still relief and release.

After Christopher Reeve suffered a horseback riding accident in 1995, he was not only paralyzed, but had a feeding tube and a breathing device. For some time, so much of life seemed lost to him. However, he later spoke of sitting on his deck and looking out over the beauty of the countryside. He said in spite of everything, he was amazed how much was still left.

It is miraculous and wonderful for us to think about the many things that we have even when so much seems to have been taken away from us. I have been amazed that in spite of this problem, I still have a caring husband, a very comfortable and lovely home, an adorable cat, the beauty of the scenery where I live, and good friends. I have been able to continue working at a job that I love. I'm also fully aware of people who have far more physical and mental problems than I do. And yet, one might list the blessings that come in spite of the deficiencies. I expect all of us can find some blessings. Life has so many riches to offer us so even when some are taken away from us, there is still much left "in spite of."

Some years ago, after I had grown up, my mother said to me, "I always wanted my girls to feel that life was good. I wanted you to be exposed to good things and to good experiences." We have the possibility in our illnesses to actually see more deeply into life. On the one hand, we undoubtedly see more deeply into the woundedness and the brokenness of life. We certainly are experiencing it day by day and hour by hour, but it is also possible to see more deeply into the goodness of life. There is so much that is beautiful in creation, just looking at the sea or the mountains or the trees or the birds. Sometimes our illness opens us up to something in life that we might not have seen that is good and rich and even profound.

My audio therapy included listening to Mozart for 30 minutes every morning and to environmental sounds for 20 to 30 minutes every night. I grew up with classical music, which included playing piano and flute, and I've certainly listened to Mozart and even played Mozart before this illness. But since I had been asked by my doctors to listen to Mozart, I found a new richness in music. Mozart's melodies are charming, beautifully structured, uplifting at times, and at other times meditative. His harmonies are lovely and the music is quite broad, from playful to somber to rich and inspiring. Without this illness, of course, I could still listen to Mozart, but would I have listened to the same extent?

Another of my therapies has included aromatherapy, specifically sniffing peppermint during the day every once in a while and sniffing lavender at night. My doctor told me this is good for the brain, so I do it. Sometimes in my doctor's office and particularly in the clinic, I have smelled the rich, spicy smell of cloves as some other patient is sniffing their therapy. Of course, I can sniff peppermint and lavender without being ill, but would I have?

Part of my therapy involved going to the pool several times a week and doing exercises in the warm water—I was surprised how much I enjoyed the water and the interaction among other people exercising. Of course, I could do this without my illness, but I didn't.

Part of the "in spite of" has to do with these things that come to us because of our efforts or remain as blessings in spite of our illness. Our illness has the potential to let us see more deeply and more clearly how much there is in life. Whether we experience something additional in life, such as certain therapies we enjoy or certain people we meet, or whether our illness helps us acknowledge those things that we still have in spite of illness, we might say with Christopher Reeve, "I'm surprised how much there still is."

CHAPTER 30:

Waiting For A Miracle

Each day is a different one, each day
brings a miracle of its own. It's just a matter
of paying attention to this miracle.
—Paulo Coelho

There is a fine line between expecting a miracle, and being true to the process of healing. We all want something to happen very quickly. We want to think that overnight there will be this miraculous moment of healing. We want to believe in the possibility of such a miracle. But it can be just as important for us to stay in the process while still waiting for that moment.

There is a term that is called "the suspension of disbelief." The suspension of disbelief means that we're willing to put aside our disbelief in the possibility of something wonderful and miraculous happening, or not happening. It doesn't mean that we expect miracles to happen, nor do we take for granted a miracle won't happen. We're open to it if it comes, but are willing to stay with the slow healing process if it doesn't.

This idea is often used in theater because, when we enter the theater, we *suspend our disbelief* and act *as if* what we're watching is real. We engage with the play and believe in what's happening for the length of the play. At the end of the play, we go back to our reality, but we have suspended our disbelief during that period of time.

In the early years of my business, I worked with a marketing director who told me she considered the ability to suspend our disbelief was one of the most important qualities for success. If we believe we don't deserve success (or healing,) or if we believe a miracle can't happen to us, then we don't have the faith necessary to allow something good to happen which would change our reality. We become disbelievers, putting up barriers and not allowing God to work according to His purpose.

In a sense, we need to live during our illness with the suspension of disbelief. We don't know what will happen, but we're open to all possibilities without clinging to one expectation.

St. Bernadette had a vision of the Virgin Mary in France in the 1800s at a place named Lourdes where a stream started to flow. The stream had miraculous powers for some people, and it is said that many people were healed by these flowing waters.

After Bernadette left the area, she developed a very bad ulcer in her leg. The nuns at her convent asked her to journey back to allow these waters to heal her, believing that since it had healed others it would automatically heal her.

Bernadette said that the waters were not for her. She felt she would not be healed by the waters, in spite of the fact that others were. This seemed so odd to me when I first heard it. Yet, her story inspired me. It helped me accept the fact that miracles are not automatically given just because we pray often and fervently. A miracle may or may not be for us. Even saints get ill, suffer, and die.

In our illness, we would like to be the person who is struck by the miraculous healing power of God. Suddenly everything would be changed because healing has come into our lives and, of all people, we would be the ones who are blessed. But sometimes it's not to be. So we stand between the suspension of disbelief, recognizing that there could be a miracle, but also recognizing that perhaps that miracle is not for us and that we have to simply stay in the process. We recognize a miracle may or may not happen, but we know if we stop hoping for a miracle we would feel abandoned and lose hope. So we keep ourselves open to the possibility—suspended between belief and disbelief.

CHAPTER 31:

The Third Day Always Comes

Jesus said, "On the third day I will reach my goal."
—Luke 13:32

And the angel said, "He has risen, just as He said."
—Matthew 28:6

When I was in high school, my sister heard this saying: "The third day always comes." Easter follows Good Friday. We learned to say it in our family when things went wrong and we weren't sure when they would go right again. We might need to go to the Garden of Gethsemane where we're asked to accept what is happening, even though we hoped that events would take another direction. There might then be a crucifixion of great suffering we need to go through before the resurrection.

Like Jesus, we might also go down into our own metaphorical hell. In the Apostles Creed, it is said that Jesus descended into hell, where He freed the good people who had died before He came. He had suffered and died for their sins, as well as for the sins of those living and those who were to come. While He was in hell, He overcame the devil and brought the good people from the darkness into the light.

While we're in the depths, we have the opportunity to look around, see what needs to be fixed, and then return to help others because we've "been there and done that." We no longer have the same fear of The Darkness because we have prevailed and have returned. Jesus has redeemed us from the darkest of all forces.

Within the Christian faith, there is a belief in the miracle of The Third Day. The Resurrection happens. Christ is risen indeed. There is an Easter Sunday after there is a Good Friday. Darkness and blackness lead to light. Everything that seems to have been wrong and coming to an end rises to something much better.

The ability to believe in the "third day" doesn't always mean that the third day comes on the third day. Sometimes the third day comes a month later, five years later, ten years later, or perhaps not until the release of death. Hope eventually finds a reason to hope.

CHAPTER 32:

Finding Amazing Grace

Through many dangers, toils and snares
We have already come
T'was grace that brought us safe thus far
And grace will lead us home.
—from the song by John Newton

Quakers focus on Experience, whether the experience of The Presence of God, or of Forgiveness, or of Reconciliation, or Experiencing The Light Within. They often ask, "What can you say from your own experience?" I have thought often of the word "Grace," but didn't really understand it experientially. I understood Blessings—being given great gifts by God that fulfill our souls and make us whole and make us capable of giving. I understood Forgiveness and The Light Within and Transformation. But Grace was something I studied, but never really felt.

In December 2015, after my doctor analyzed my cancer cell, she told me I didn't have to have chemotherapy since my cancer cell was low risk. I first felt an outpouring of gratitude to God. "Thank you, thank you, thank you!" And gratitude for all the prayers and support I received. But then I felt as if I was bathed in something sweet and light and loving. I believe I felt the power of God's grace. I stopped to try to put a word to it and I thought of the word, "Reprieve." I expected I'd have to walk this difficult path and had accepted that this would be how it would go. And then, suddenly, I was reprieved. I felt as if I was released. I was let off the hook.

Of course, we call that salvation or unmerited favor, and in a bigger sense, we're always under God's Eternal Saving Grace. But I was able to differentiate God's blessings (the gifts we receive) from the Enveloping Taken-Care-Of Reprieve of Amazing Grace.

CHAPTER 33:

And What Have We Learned

*Experience is a teacher and here's
what makes me burn. She's always teaching me the
things I do not care to learn.*
(Profound wisdom I learned as a child, from
"Grin and Bear It" by Michael Moore, a column of
Boy's Life, February 1967.)

We might substitute the word "illness" for the word "experience." We might think of our illness as teaching us what we don't want to learn, but I sometimes wonder if our illness actually teaches us something that we do want to learn, but we've had trouble learning in any other way.

Since my early 20s, I've always wanted to be more compassionate. I felt I was creative and I was positive and I had some other good traits, but one of the traits that I most admired in other people was compassion. It didn't seem to come naturally to me. This was partly because my life had been dedicated to creativity and spirituality and helping to nurture those qualities in other people. So I didn't have a motivating force of compassion determining my life's work.

My illness has put me far more in contact with other people who are ill. At the doctors' offices and at the physical therapy center, I saw people with amputated legs and with MS and people in wheelchairs and with canes and with limps and with severely painful conditions. I saw people that had certain deformities that I have not witnessed before, and people who had difficulties and problems in their joints and in their bones. We often talked. We might not have always talked about our diseases and illnesses or injuries, but we did talk. I found many of these people to be of great faith in spite of their illness. I saw how courageously and with what patience they dealt with the limits that their illness has caused them. I began to be more sensitive, not just of them, but of people on the street or at the mall or at a church who were struggling in one way or another. I was surprised at their positive attitudes, since I expected anyone with an illness or disease to be continually depressed. Not true.

My husband works in the healing profession as an acupuncturist and a massage therapist. He's a very compassionate person. Certainly, some of his attitudes have rubbed off on me in the over 30 years that we've been married. I've been able to apply one of the things I've learned from him, which is a kind of "matter of fact" accepting way of dealing with people that have various physical problems. Peter is very direct and is also very accepting. He doesn't shy away from asking personal questions and many people seem to like to talk about their difficulties since other people try to ignore them or think it would be embarrassing to ask. Of course, none of us wants to talk all the time about our problems, but I have found there is something kind and accepting when someone asks me a question and shows sensitivity and understanding. Physical problems are not something to shy away from. They're part of the totality of who we are at this point in our lives. To pretend they don't exist is to not see us clearly. We can pretend they shouldn't be there or pretend they're not so bad or pretend that if we only prayed a little harder and had a few more positive thoughts they would go away, but pretending gets us no place.

I think of how often it is said in the Bible that Jesus had compassion for the many people that were brought to him with various diseases. He also had compassion for humanity. He knew well what it was like to be human.

In these years of my illness, I have also begun to recognize that almost all of us have some things in our lives that are difficult, that we struggle with, that threaten to overwhelm us, that get in the way of good things. We see some of these problems as we look at a person, but some of them are quite well hidden and we might never know that they exist.

Sometimes I speak at a Christian conference where I met a woman named Vonda Skelton. She's an author and international speaker and she is absolutely adorable and so positive and so lovely that she just shines with light. At one of these conferences, I was watching her and I said to myself, "Now that's one person who doesn't have things in her life that she has to deal with." She seemed so radiant and so happy all the time that I made a presumption about her situation. A day later, Vonda and I got together to talk. I wanted to tell her that I had cervical dystonia and how I was struggling with it. As we were walking together down the path, Vonda said to me, "Could you please walk on my left side because I'm almost deaf in my right ear. When I was a child I had Ménière's disease which caused this problem." That broke through my attitude that said, "Some people just have it really good and they don't have these things in their lives like I have." My new attitude is, "Almost *everybody* has things to deal with!" One way or another, we're all in the same boat.

CHAPTER 34:

Getting Through, Getting Beyond

It's healthy to say uncle when your bone's about to break.
—Jonathan Franzen, *How to Be Alone*

"There are things in life you just have to get through," said one of my doctors. There are times the rough and tough stuff that makes up a part of our life is so overwhelming, that we simply have to put one foot in front of the other. We don't need to put any added pressure on ourselves to do it well or gracefully or lovingly. Just do it.

There were days I realized I wasn't being particularly nice or generous or caring. I wasn't a good listener. I wasn't being compassionate about the other person's problems. I simply had to cope. I didn't have to like it, but I did have to get through it.

But I found as I surmounted those things I had to surmount—doctor's appointments, going daily to radiation for 20 days, doing exercises, and getting through it—that it was time to Get Beyond it. Yes, I had gotten through it. But now, there's the next step.

During the Getting Through times, there isn't a whole lot of time for reflection, or self–improvement exercises, or looking at our behavior or attitudes to work on becoming a better and more likable person. That sometimes has to wait. Even God doesn't get His well-deserved time. Prayers are often short because we don't have the energy for long talks with God. We depend on the prayers from friends to keep us lifted up and moving forward. Mainly, we do what we need to do.

During these times, I found myself easily irritated, stumbling yet trying to get back on my feet, and looking for my Lost Center. But I didn't have time to stop by the Lost and Found to see if Center was stuck there. As the stuff of illness began to heal a bit, I wondered how to make this all mean something. I noticed that cancer sharpened my mind, working like a laser to pinpoint those parts in my life I wanted to change and those parts where I needed an attitude adjustment. I didn't want to just leave it behind and forget about it or pretend it hadn't happened. I wanted to get to the summit of the mountain without losing track of the hard work I had done to get there.

I presumed, that to get beyond and to get to some higher or deeper or better level, I had to change myself. But I began to think that getting beyond might not always mean just that. It certainly didn't mean changing others to fit my needs, but it did seem important to think about the irritants and stresses in my life that I needed to get rid of. There were some things in life I was better without. True, the Enlightened Being could put up with everything with a quiet mind and inner peace, but I wasn't that enlightened and I didn't need to put that trip on myself as well. I reflected on my working relationships—some of them wonderful, others that just didn't work for me. I realized that things and certain people bothered me. I told myself, "Don't presume that you always have to change yourself. Maybe you have to admit what works, and what doesn't work for you." If it doesn't work, there's no need to cling to it. Let it go.

Letting Go was always hard for me. I thought I had to resolve everything and get along. Some things did need to be resolved and I tried to resolve them and then determined not to get entangled with that person or that stressor again. No—just let it go.

Going Beyond is sometimes a time of cutting strings. Sometimes it's a matter of changing how we use our time. Sometimes it's resituating ourselves to what is important in our day. We're re-setting the clock. Adjusting the shades so we know how best to let the sunshine in. We're trying to be more self-directed rather than other-directed. If someone tells us what they believe to be true, we can decide whether it's true for us.

How do we learn to be a singing instrument even if we're not the most perfect instrument in the orchestra of life? Where are relationships and actions tuned well and where do they need to be sharper so we don't live downtrodden and flat? Where are the keepers in our lives and what is the stuff we should give to Goodwill?

We can practice doing Small Snippet Prayers. "Oh, God, this is so tiring! Help!" Or "I don't like myself when I do this—give me a bit of leeway and help me change this behavior!" Or "Give me the strength to go on tomorrow because I'm all worn out for today!"

We can Go Beyond by apologizing for crossing boundaries and being snippy and snarky. Or, for not being able to give at a time we can't even give to ourselves, much less to others. We can re-set that little dial that tells us "You've gone too far" and decide to try to better drive, and color, within the lines. We can occasionally use the excuse "the cancer" (or fill in the disease) "made me do it," but that excuse can only be used a few times. On the other hand, it is the truth.

Sometimes creative angst and letting it rip and spilling our guts on someone else's floor is not the best way to go. And sometimes, that's just how it spilled out and now we have to mop up, fess up, and take a step higher. And hopefully then, higher still.

We might decide we haven't gone far enough and we need to be a bit spontaneous and add some color to our lives. We want to integrate the tough climb into our lives and then hopefully, not be afraid to sit in the sunshine at the summit, accept the scars and scratches and bruises, and tell ourselves that we were courageous, determined, and we persevered. Yay for us! We Got Through and we're Moving Beyond!

CHAPTER 35:

Planning The Celebration

Thou who art...May I thank Thee for all that shall fall to
my lot.., May everything in this ...
be directed to Thy glory
And may I never despair For I am under Thy hand
And in Thee is all power and goodness.
—Dag Hammarskjold

We often have an expectation that when we're healed it's going to be great. There's going to be that miraculous moment when everything is now all right and we're back to normal. It's easy to celebrate when it's all over. But the little steps need to be celebrated as well. Sometimes it's the ability to take a walk when we haven't been able to walk for some months. Sometimes it's the ability to get out and have a normal day. Or we feel good and we suddenly want to go to a concert or play. Sometimes it's the ability to do a therapy or an exercise that we weren't able to do before, or

153

the ability to do it better. Sometimes our eyes are open to the beauty of nature and we begin to notice birds singing and the trees blooming and the flowers are perking up.

Sometimes it's the enjoyment of music or a taste of something we haven't enjoyed for quite some time. We might celebrate the end of chemotherapy, going home again after a long hospital stay, the first anniversary of some improvement, the last day of rehabilitation, the first time the bandages are removed, getting through the operation—something is always worth celebrating! We re-engage and reach out to life again after a long hibernation that tells us that we're on a road to healing.

In my case, I finished with the cancer treatment and celebrated with my husband and friends. Well wishes and flowers abounded! The Cancer Center also has their own celebration when the patients complete their treatment. The patient rings a gong three times and recites a little verse, "This is a day of celebration as you continue on your Life's Journey... Reflect on the accomplishment of meeting the challenges that have come your way... Striking the gong three times signifies: Letting Go of The Past, Living in The Present, Embracing The Future. We honor you and wish you peace."

Since I'm not finished with my treatments for dystonia, one of my goals has been to recognize and find, even if for just moments, what "Center" is. For me, my first celebration happened when I closed my eyes, my head reached center and then stayed there for some moments. Reaching center doesn't mean that it's all healed, because I have to reach center and have it *stay there* as opposed to it resting at center for only some moments. But, it was an important moment. I drank a glass of champagne with a friend and bought my doctor a ceramic cupcake!

Afterword

Dr. Gail Henry

I have had the honor and privilege of being one member of Linda's healthcare team and part of that support circle for her. Each one of us have specialized training and unique roles in her rehabilitation. Our specialty is in rehabilitation of physical and neurological disorders including dystonia. The physical pain of constant forceful muscle spasms forcing the head, neck, shoulders, spine, pelvis or lower extremities into an unnatural position that cannot be voluntarily stopped is not only physically disabling to various degrees but is also very emotionally disturbing to those afflicted. Loss of self-esteem, overwhelming self-consciousness or embarrassment, and an inability to perform or enjoy normal activities of daily living are suffered by many with dystonia. Linda has not experienced all of these problems, but has been in touch a number of times sharing her discouragement and yet telling me she had managed to stave off depression.

As you read Linda's book on her reflections and meditations during her journey of actively seeking God's healing, searching and finding those of us in the healthcare profession who are God's instruments to help His beloved people, you met a very remarkable woman and were treated to her deep insight and her personal love for people. When in Linda's presence, you are in the presence of someone who very naturally extends genuine love and kindness. Linda makes anyone and everyone feel like they are the most special person in all the world. She is also the most giving person I have ever met. The ceramic cupcake to celebrate being able to hold her head center for a few moments at a time is only one of many love gifts from her to me and to our staff. Linda truly loves people and has a capacity to reach out and make new friends all over the country, all over the world, bringing her glow of happiness with her. Although she has a serious neurological disorder that has changed her life, has brought times of discouragement and sadness, her inner joy has not been stolen and she shines with that even during low moments. She loves life and is more active in enjoying it then most people and most people do not have a serious neurological disorder.

I was very deeply touched and honored when she referred to me as "Sophia", "her wisdom". I smiled, too, because if anyone is wise, it is Linda. Linda is astutely intelligent and well renowned nationally and internationally. She thrives on her work because it brings her joy, not for the fame. She has more courage, strength, determination, love, vitality and wisdom than can be shared in words.

As the gifted writer she is, she was able to share the core of who we are, what we need on our individual journeys through life and all the valleys or low points that we may encounter. Faith in God and His infinite love for us, support from our loved ones, our friends, and the experts in any field that we may need expert help from. She captures the deep inner need of us humans in sharing her personal story.

Linda has shown considerable improvement in the rotatory cervical dystonia she has suffered from and her journey continues with continued signs of viable central neurons that modulate the involuntary contractions. She has not reached a state of maximum recovery that we hope and expect to reach with her. It is a blessing and privilege to just know Linda and an honor to be part of her healthcare team.

I would like to share how Dr. David Jeremiah of Turning Point Radio and Television Ministries speaks about faith:

"Faith is not passive but active. It does something.
Faith brings the proper sacrifice.
Faith enables one to walk with God.
Faith builds an ark when it has never rained.
Faith goes out not knowing where it's going.
Faith dwells in tents in a foreign country.
Faith looks for a city whose builder and maker is God.
Faith receives strength to bear a child when the mother is past the age of child bearing.
Faith offers up one's own son in obedience.
Faith believes in the resurrection.
Faith promises not to leave Jacob's bones in Egypt.
Faith refuses to be called the son of Pharaoh's daughter.
Faith chooses to suffer affliction with the people of God.
Faith esteems the reproach of Christ greater riches then the treasures of Egypt.
Faith forsakes Egypt for the promised land.
Faith passes through the Red Sea as on dry ground.

Faith walks around Jericho until the walls fall down.
Faith subdues kingdoms.
Faith works righteousness, obtains promises.
Faith stops the mouths of Lions.
Faith quenches the violence of fire.
Faith escapes the edge of the sword.
Faith turns flight to the enemies of aliens.
Faith receives the dead back to life
And Faith receives the Promise.

Faith does something."

Faith Always Does Something, even if internal and not external. That is the greatest miracle of all—what faith does internally. Who we become versus who we were. What a miracle from a loving God to us. Linda shares her deep personal relationship with God the Father, Jesus, the Holy Spirit in a way that makes us want to have wall talks with Jesus and walk through the garden with Him. How very special. How very sacred. May our Holy Trinity continue to help us help Linda and answer our prayers for her full recovery.

About The Author

Linda Seger is a seminary graduate with a Th.D. in Theology and Drama, an M.A. in Religion and the Arts, an M.A. in Feminist Theology, and an M.A. in Drama. She grew up Lutheran, has attended many other denominations over the years, and is a member of Colorado Springs Friends Meeting (Quakers). Linda has been a script consultant in the film industry since 1981, has given seminars and lectures in over 30 countries around the world, and is the author of 14 books including the best selling screenwriting book, *Making a Good Script Great.* She lives in the Rocky Mountains near Colorado Springs with her dear husband and a magnificent cat!